OPTIMIZING PERFORMANCE IN DB2™ SOFTWARE

Prentice Hall Mainframe Software Series

*The CICS Companion: A Reference Guide to COBOL Command Level
 Programming*, by Thomas R. Gildersleeve
OS and VS Job Control Language and Utility Programs, Second Edition,
 by Daniel H. Rindfleisch
Using VAX/VMS, by Essential Resources, Inc. (ERI) with Jan Diamondstone
CICS/VS Command Level Programming with COBOL Examples, by David Lee
IMS/VS DB/DC Online Programming Using MFS and DL/1, by David Lee
IMS/VS DL/1 Programming with COBOL Examples, by David Lee
CICS/VS Online System Design and Implementation Techniques, by David Lee
VSAM Coding in COBOL and VSAM AMS, by David Lee

OPTIMIZING PERFORMANCE IN DB2™ SOFTWARE

W. H. Inmon
American Management Systems

PRENTICE HALL

Englewood Cliffs, New Jersey 07632

Library of Congress Cataloging-in-Publication Data

Inmon, William H.
    Optimizing performance in DB2 software.

    Bibliography: p.
    Includes index.
    1. Data base management.   2. IBM Database 2 (Computer
system)   I. Title.
QA76.9.D3I543   1988   005.75′65   88-2414
ISBN 0-13-638230-4

Editorial/production supervision: Chris Baumle, Editing, Design and Production, Inc.
Cover design: Ben Santora
Manufacturing buyer: Mary Ann Gloriande
DB2 is a trademark of International Business Machines Corp.

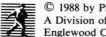

The publisher offers discounts on this book when ordered in bulk quantities. For more information,
write:

  Special Sales/College Marketing
  Prentice Hall
  College Technical and Reference Division
  Englewood Cliffs, NJ 07632

Printed in the United States of America

10 9 8 7 6 5 4 3 2

ISBN 0-13-638230-4

PRENTICE-HALL INTERNATIONAL (UK) LIMITED, *London*
PRENTICE-HALL OF AUSTRALIA PTY. LIMITED, *Sydney*
PRENTICE-HALL CANADA INC., *Toronto*
PRENTICE-HALL HISPANOAMERICANA, S.A., *Mexico*
PRENTICE-HALL OF INDIA PRIVATE LIMITED, *New Delhi*
PRENTICE-HALL OF JAPAN, INC., *Tokyo*
SIMON & SCHUSTER ASIA PTE. LTD., *Singapore*
EDITORA PRENTICE-HALL DO BRASIL, LTDA., *Rio de Janeiro*

For my good friend, Ernie Riddle

Contents

SECTION II
DB2 Application Design

REFERENCES

INDEX

Preface

IBM's DB2 product is a powerful tool with many capabilities and numerous possibilities. DB2 can be used by the end user, programmer, manager, decision support analyst—indeed, a wide community of users. DB2 has so many options that it can be the DBMS to suit nearly all data base processing needs across a wide spectrum of users.

One very special usage of DB2 is the focus of this book: DB2 as a tool for production, online applications. Although DB2 has many other legitimate uses, this book will focus almost entirely on DB2 in the production, online environment.

The issues of production, online processing begin with performance and availability. *Performance* refers to the amount of time required for a user to complete a transaction. In the production, online environment, when the system either does not perform well or is unavailable, no other facets of the system matter. Consequently, the discipline that is required of the designer to achieve high performance and availability takes precedence over other system features.

Online performance centers around the physical I/Os required to support the processing of online systems. The central issues of performance will naturally emphasize the minimization of I/O and the effective use of I/O.

I/Os are minimized by the proper construction of the production environment, by proper system design, and by proper tuning once the system has been built. This book takes the philosophy that

- if the online production environment is not properly constructed, then no amount of sound design or tuning will achieve adequate performance in the long run,
- if the application is not designed properly, then no amount of tuning will achieve adequate performance in the long run, and

- after the production, online application has properly been designed and constructed, then tuning the application provides the fine touches to enhance online performance.

The discussions in this book reflect the philosophy that satisfactory performance is created in that manner.

This book is for application designers, system programmers, data base administrators, data base designers, managers of DB2 development projects, and, in short, anyone interested in the DB2 production environment. It is divided into two sections: general data base and transaction design considerations and application-oriented considerations.

The first section discusses the DB2 environment, data base design for performance, transaction design for performance, detailed DB2 considerations, and DB2 in the batch environment. It concentrates on technology in the frame of reference of good performance and availability.

The second section addresses data structures, referential integrity, denormalization, bill of material processing, high availability systems, archival processing and DB2, and the strategic positioning of DB2 with other software. The second section more strongly relates to applications and their usage of DB2.

This book is not a replacement for the basic descriptions of the technology of DB2 that already exist in the marketplace. Instead, it is meant to supplement the body of documentation that already exists by exploring subjects not found elsewhere.

This book assumes that the reader has at least a working acquaintance with DB2 and the basic technological foundations. This book aims not to describe the technology one more time but to describe how best to use the technology.

Acknowledgments

Materially contributing to the text were Judy Grote and Bernadette Baldauf of Wells Fargo Bank, Gary Dodge of Coopers and Lybrand, and Dr. Fred Forman of American Management Systems. In addition, the day-to-day support of the American Management Systems staff has been invaluable. A sincere thanks.

W. H. Inmon

OPTIMIZING PERFORMANCE IN DB2™ SOFTWARE

ESTABLISHING THE DB2 ENVIRONMENT

CHAPTER 1
THE DB2 ENVIRONMENT

Online, Interactive Environments

The differences between online and interactive processing are germane to he larger issue of establishing the DB2 online production environment. In the online environment, there is good, consistent online response time throughout the day. Each transaction in the online environment executes—from initiation in the terminal to the processor and back to the terminal—in a matter of seconds. Performance in peak periods is consistently good in the online environment. In a non-DB2 environment, typical online software is TPF (formerly ACP).

The interactive environment combines characteristics of both the online environment and the batch environment. In the interactive environment, there typically is direct access to data and to the session manager, thus making the interactive environment appear to be online. However, the interactive environment has other characteristics as well, such as the initiation and execution of sorts, merges, compilations, and other long-running jobs. During peak periods of processing, the interactive environment takes on the characteristics of a pure batch processor. VM/CMS and TSO are examples of software used in the interactive environment.

The effectiveness of the online environment is directly proportional to the response time achieved in the environment. The business justification for the online environment is especially sensitive to online response time, especially during peak-period processing. The DB2 architect attempting to use DB2 for online processing should be very clear as to the differences between the online and interactive environments. The purpose of this book is to address the usage of DB2 in the online environment, not the interactive environment.

The DB2 Production Environment

Before the DB2 production environment can be defined and controlled, the production developer must first understand some of the basics of the DB2 environment. The three most important aspects of the environment to the production developer who desires to attain good, consistent online system performance are

- the system environment
- the execution of an SQL program
- the physical data base environment

Each of these aspects of DB2 will be described in an overview. The reader is invited to review these topics in depth in the materials cited in the bibliography.

THE SYSTEM ENVIRONMENT

Terminal access to DB2 is achieved in conjunction with IMS, CICS, and TSO. The relationship of DB2 to these standard pieces of software is depicted by Figure 1.1.

3

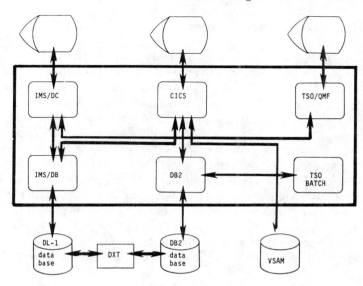

Figure 1.1

In either IMS or CICS, DB2 is accessed through SQL statements that are embedded in application code, that is, in COBOL or PL-1 code. In TSO, DB2 is accessed through the QMF facility. DB2-controlled data can also be loaded from as IMS data base by means of the DXT (Data Extract Facility). When DB2 is accessed from IMS, it is accessed only from the control region; in other words, IMS batch cannot access DB2.

Some Relevant Dynamics

An aspect of DB2 that is very important to performance is the inner dynamics of the management of data and the management of transactions. Understanding the structure and the dynamics of the DB2 components that address the protection of data and transaction integrity, the flow of events, and the usage and access of data is essential to achieving online performance. These technical issues focus on, among other things, the way DB2 manages the locking of data.

An important component of DB2 is its locking facility. Locking data prevents multiple online users from simultaneously updating the same data and creating erroneous results. Locking is an important factor in the number of online users who can access data concurrently and to online performance in general. DB2 uses the IRLM facility to manage all locks.

Locks can be held at various levels in DB2, such as tablespaces, pages, indexes, databases, and PLANs. The locking strategy for any given program is determined at the moment of BIND. Locks are held for a program as it goes into execution until a COMMIT, DEALLOCATION, or UNLOCK is issued.

The effects on performance of locking can be minimized by using two types of DB2 data bases: read-only and update data bases. Locking is absolutely minimized when a program is accessing read-only data bases. In addition to minimizing the conflicts with locks, separating data into read-only and update data bases helps minimize the underlying data management of the data bases. Read-only data can be very tightly packed because the data and its indexes never have to be modified, once created. Update data, of course, must address the issues of insertion, update, and deletion.

Other technical details relevant to DB2 online performance are:

- the management and use of indexes. Indexes can be added or deleted at any time in DB2. Indexes can be important to performance in that their existence can cause queries to use less I/O than is otherwise necessary.

- the access paths used in the location and access of data. DB2 decides internally which views and which access paths are to be used. The path is stored in a PLAN, which is used at execution time to determine the optimal method(s) to use in satisfying the calls issued by the query.

- the programs used to process against DB2 data bases. Programs that can access DB2 can be written in APL, assembler, COBOL, FORTRAN, and PL-1.

If the DB2 production environment is to achieve adequate online performance during the peak-period processing window, a certain amount of isolation of processing and data is required. This isolation is achieved through facilities such as the restricted usage of the DB2 catalog during the online day.

PROGRAM FLOW

The program flow of SQL is illustrated by Figure 1.2. Application source code is entered into a SQL precompiler. One of the outputs of the precompiler is a DBRM, which is one of the inputs—along with table definitions—to the BIND

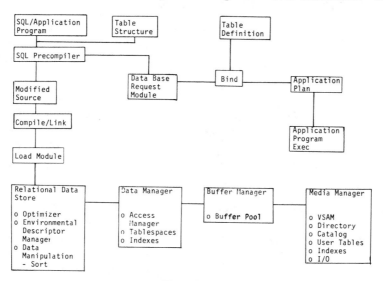

Figure 1.2

process, from which the PLAN is created, which determines the optimal access path. Modified source code is created, which is input into the compile-link process from which a load module is executed. Once execution is initiated, data requests are satisfied in the Relational Data Store (RDS).

The requests for data flow from the RDS to the data manager, which translates set requests for data into actual data base calls. From the data manager, the buffer manager is called. The buffer manager manipulates the different buffer pools. The media manager is called from the buffer manager and accesses data at the VSAM (ESDS) level.

Data are inserted into a table using either the SQL insert facility or the DB2 load utility.

Data are committed to a database at a commit point. At a commit point, the updates can be considered to be permanent. (Of course, prior to a commit point, the data base updates can be backed out.)

The actual commit point depends upon the terminal access method in which the program is running. In IMS, for example, a commit point could be a SYNC point, or a CHKP checkpoint.

PHYSICAL STRUCTURES

The lowest unit of information in DB2 is the field. A field is defined by the data base designer-administrator at the moment of physical data base design. A single field exists for a single row. For multiple rows, the same fields in each row form a column. Fields contain the occurrence of a data element. For example, if a field name were a part number, the field might contain the value of a part number—1245pg.

DB2 gives the designer four physical formats for a field:

- fixed length, no null values allowed
- fixed length, null values allowed
- variable length, no null values allowed
- variable length, null values allowed

If a field can have null values, there is a prefix for the field. Figure 1.3 shows the different possibilities for field definitions.

In Figure 1.3 a *P* in the prefix for a field indicates the field contents are present, and an *N* indicates the contents are null. If a field cannot have null values, there is no field prefix for it. If a field is variable in length, it has a prefix indicating the length of the field. Note that a variable-length field that is not null may have a length of zero, which is the logical equivalent of being null.

Fields are defined into rows or tuples. A row is a group of related fields whose existence depends upon the key of the row. As an example, a row for a bank account activity might have a key of ACCOUNT/ACTIVITY DATE/ACTIVITY TIME and nonkey fields such as AMOUNT, LOCATION, TELLER, and PERSONAL IDENTIFICATION. Rows can be fixed length or variable length. If a row contains only fixed-length fields, then the row is fixed in length.

| abcdefghij..... | Fixed field length, no nulls allowed

| P | abcdefgh.... | | N | ----------- | Fixed length fields, null values allowed

| 1 | abcdefgh.... | Variable length fields, no nulls allowed

| 1 | P | abcdefg... | | 1 | N | Variable length fields, null values allowed

Figure 1.3 The types of fields supported by DB2.

If a row contains one or more variable-length fields, then the row is variable in length. Rows are combined together into pages. Figure 1.4 illustrates rows and pages.

The page shown in Figure 1.4 shows ten tuples and three unused spaces· where future tuples may be placed. The rows have a primary key—employee number—and four nonkey fields—hire date, starting salary, starting location, and supervisor. For a row to exist, only the primary key must exist. Other nonkey fields may be present or null. A page is either 4k bytes or 32k bytes in length. If a page is 32k bytes, it is made up of eight 4k byte VSAM control intervals, or CIs, as shown in Figure 1.5.

Rows fit entirely within a page, that is, rows do not span from one page to the next. DB2 data bases are defined to VSAM exclusively.

Employee Number	Hire Date	Starting Salary	Starting Location	Supervisor
1908	Jun2183	--	Tallahassee	G Jones
2807	Aug0176	530	Shreveport	T Wynette
--	--	--	--	--
--	--	--	--	--
0019	Sep1765	980	Jackson	W Nelson
--	--	--	--	--
1007	Jan0166	500	--	G Jones
1108	Dec1580	--	Dallas	G Jones
1507	Jul2086	975	Shreveport	--
1807	Aug2184	1000	Oxford	G Jones
2106	Jul1979	997	--	T Wynette
0078	Feb2886	1065	Miami	W Nelson
1004	Aug2380	--	Gatlinburg	W Jennings

Figure 1.4 A page is made up of rows, or tuples. A tuple is made up of fields. The primary key for this page (or table) is employee number. Note that nonkey data may exist for any field except for the primary key, but for a tuple to exist, the key must exist. Also note that any field may be a foreign key.

```
CREATE TABLE EMPL
            ( EMPNO        CHAR(8)          NOT NULL,
              HIREDATE     CHAR(6)          NOT NULL,
              STARTSAL     DECIMAL(7,2)    NOT NULL,
              STARTLOC     VARCHAR(24)     NOT NULL,
              SUPERVIS     VARCHAR(24))
            IN DATABASE XXXXXXX;
```

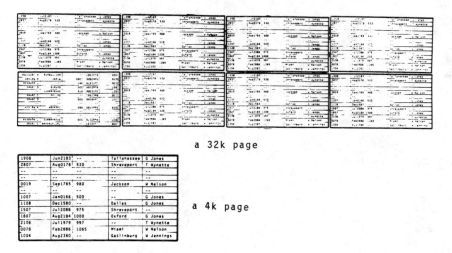

a 32k page

a 4k page

Figure 1.5   Each ci is 4k bytes.

Rows can be added or deleted one at a time, or they can be loaded and deleted en masse. Columns can be added to a row after the row is defined, but even if the added column is fixed in length, the row is defined as variable in length. When a row is deleted, the space is marked as reusable. The space can be reused for the occurrence of another row or for the extension of an existing variable-length row.

Pages are arranged into table spaces. Table spaces come in two forms: simple table spaces and partitioned table spaces. A simple table space can hold several types of tables together or a single table. A partitioned table space holds only one type of table, but the table is divided into 2 to 64 units called *partitions,* as shown in Figure 1.6.

Simple table spaces are good for small, interrelated tables; partitioned tables are good for large tables.

Data is organized into pages either randomly or sequentially. If the data is stored randomly, it is said to be *nonclustered.* Data stored sequentially is said

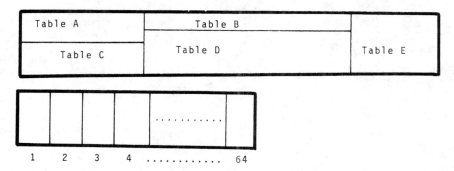

Figure 1.6   (*a*) A simple table space made up of pages for several types of tables; (*b*) a partitioned table space.

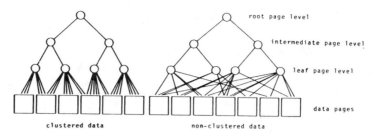

Figure 1.7   The index structure of DB2.

to be *clustered*. Whether clustered or nonclustered, there can be zero or more indexes pointing to designated fields. The index has three levels: the root page level, the intermediate page level, and the leaf page level. The two top levels of indexes are used to point to the leaf pages in much the same way as master indexes are used to point to data in other systems.

The leaf pages actually point to the pages where rows reside. A direct access into the data base uses three levels of indexing, but sequential access uses only the leaf page. If the data are clustered, the leaf page points to rows within a page and to rows in another page when the sequential order of the rows is interrupted by the physical boundaries of a page. However, when data is not clustered, the leaf pages point to data in a random fashion. Figure 1.7 illustrates clustered and nonclustered indexes.

The pointer from the leaf page to the data page is in the form of a page entry. The first part of the index pointer indicates the page at which the row can be found. The entry is accessed to find the actual location of the row within the page. This indirect pointing to data allows data management to occur within the physical page without affecting the values in the index. For example, a row can be moved from one location to another within the page, and all that must be changed is the value of the location within the page. No index manipulation is necessary. The arrangement of indexes pointing into data is shown by Figure 1.8.

TABLE RELATIONSHIPS

Tables are related to each other in DB2 by means of foreign keys. A *foreign key* is merely a field in a table that is likewise contained in another table and allows the two tables to be joined. Figure 1.9 shows a simple example of two tables related by a foreign key.

Figure 1.9 shows that customer and account tables are related by means of the account number appearing in the customer table. In this case the account for M Robbins is shown to be 1250JA, which relates to the second account shown in the account table. Note that in the structuring of data shown in the example, a customer can have only one account. If more than one account per customer is desired, a structuring of data as shown in Figure 1.10 is necessary.

In either Figure 1.9 or Figure 1.10, easy access exists only from customer to account. The reverse direction—from account to customer—is not accommo-

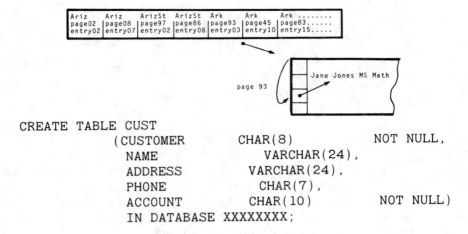

```
CREATE TABLE CUST
          (CUSTOMER        CHAR(8)              NOT NULL,
           NAME            VARCHAR(24),
           ADDRESS         VARCHAR(24),
           PHONE           CHAR(7),
           ACCOUNT         CHAR(10)             NOT NULL)
           IN DATABASE XXXXXXXX;
```

Figure 1.8 An index pointing to a page and an offset within the page. To access the first index occurrence for Arkansas, page 93 is located and the third entry in the prefix is used to actually locate the row that is being pointed to.

dated easily by the structure shown in the example. Only if there is an index on account number, making account number directly accessible, is reverse access easily done.

The foreign key relationships in DB2 are actuated by application code (with the exception of DB2 views, which will be discussed later). The programmer must be aware of the relationships between data bases and must actively build the relationships through application code.

Customer	Name	Address	Phone	Account
459701872	M Robbins	123 Heaven Gate	777-1430	1250JA
570181760	J C Riley	1 Fast Lane	841-7781	16072
774182110	L Lynn	14 Jaybird	291-6604	17011B

Account	Date Opened	Balance	Domiciling Branch	
1901K	Jul2081	1000.00	Oakland	
1250JA	Aug1376	596.42	Pinole	two tables connected by
1742AR	Mar1271	10513.13	Alameda	account number

```
CREATE TABLE ACCT
          (ACCOUNT         CHAR(10)             NOT NULL,
           DTOPENED        CHAR(6),
           BALANCE         DECIMAL(7,2),
           DOMBRANCH       CHAR(2))
           IN DATABASE XXXXXXXX;
```

Figure 1.9 Two tables connected by account number.

Customer	Name	Address	Phone
459701872	M Robbins	123 Heaven Gate	777-1430
570181760	J C Riley	1 Fast Lane	841-7781
774182110	L Lynn	14 Jaybird	291-6604
:	:	:	:

Account	Date Opened	Balance	Domiciling Branch
1901K	Jul2081	1000.00	Oakland
1250JA	Aug1376	596.42	Pinole
1742AR	Mar1271	10513.13	Alameda
:	:	:	:

Customer/Account Cross Reference

002334123	8809TR
002334123	89110K
002349817	0116P
002349820	9008GT
002349820	90122I
:	:

Figure 1.10 Three tables interconnected by a cross-reference table linking customers and accounts.

SEPARATION OF AD HOC PROCESSING

To achieve good, consistent response time in the DB2 environment, it is necessary to separate short-running activities (such as normal online transactions) from long-running activities (such as ad hoc queries or relational joins and projects). In the same view, workloads whose resource consumption is predictable need to be separated from workloads whose resource consumption is unpredictable.

When long-running and short-running activities are allowed to mix with each other, the system runs at the speed of the slowest activity. It is thus essential that the DB2 production environment be properly configured before any online application and development begins. Figure 1.11 shows the different possibilities for environmental configurations.

In state 1 in Figure 1.11, ad hoc and production activities are run together in the same machine on the same data at the same time. As long as the total ad hoc and online activity is very light, there is no need to separate the different types of activities. However, in the face of any significant amount of activity at all (as is typical of the production environment), performance degrades quickly.

In state 2 in Figure 1.11, ad hoc activities are run during nonpeak processing hours, and production processing is run during peak-period processing hours (usually during the workday). This configuration allows DB2 to achieve its maximum performance during peak-period processing hours, but restricts the access of the end user doing DB2 processing to off-hours.

In state 3 in Figure 1.11, ad hoc activities can be done during the daytime, and production processing can likewise be done during peak-period processing hours, but processing is done on separate machines. Of course, data must be periodically refreshed from the production to the ad hoc environment. Nevertheless, in this state optimum performance can be achieved and ad hoc activities can be run during the daytime.

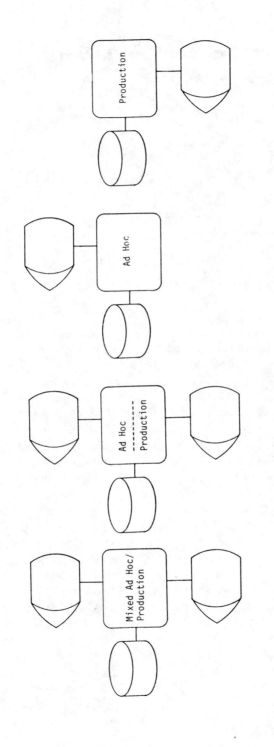

State 1

Ad hoc and production ac-
tivities are mixed in the
same processor at the same
time. This configuration
yields good performance
only when there is a very
light load of activities.

State 2

Ad hoc activities are run during
off-peak hours while production
activities are run during the
peak period processing hours. In
such a fashion the same data can
be used to serve both environments.

State 3

Ad hoc activities are run on one
machine and production activities
are run on another. Different data
serves each environment, but there
is no conflict in peak period
processing.

Figure 1.11

ENVIRONMENTAL CHARACTERISTICS

In state 2 and state 3 in Figure 1.11, the production online environment is separated from the ad hoc environment. It is in the production online environment that DB2 will achieve its highest levels of online performance. What, then, are the characteristics of the DB2 production environment?

1. No QMF access to data will be allowed. Only embedded SQL through either IMS or CICS will be allowed.
2. Only limited DXT processing will be allowed. Certain periods, such as from noon to 1:00 P.M. will be held open for DXT processing. Otherwise, DXT processing will not be allowed until peak-period transaction processing is completed.
3. No access to DB2 data will be allowed other than through the standard TP monitors.
4. All embedded SQL transactions will be designed. Chapter 3 contains a complete explanation of what is meant by *designed*. (The terminology *designed* is somewhat artificial and is used to describe the way an online transaction must be configured. The terminology has a specific meaning in the context of this book. Other terminology for the same concept might be *calibrated* or *online specific*.)
5. No data base alterations—modification or creations of indexes, additions of columns, or the like—will be allowed during the peak period for transaction processing.
6. All SQL commands used for production online processing will be precompiled.
7. Only limited views of data will be allowed for production online processing. The views allowed will be only for physical subsets of a table, not for views spanning one or more tables.
8. No sorting will be allowed during peak-period transaction processing.
9. No utilities will be run during peak-period processing hours.

PRODUCTION ONLINE ENVIRONMENT

During peak-period processing, the activities that are run are optimized for transactions moving through the system efficiently. Such is the discipline required to achieve adequate, consistent performance. However, there are facets of the production online environment other than transaction processing. After peak-period processing, DB2 is allowed to process all activities otherwise disallowed. In such a fashion the complete needs for data base processing are accomplished.

Nonpeak processing turns into the traditional batch window in which lengthy batch processes are run without interfering with production online transaction processing. Typically a batch window is during off-peak processing hours. One of the tasks of the designer is to determine how much batch window processing is to be done and what resources are required. If more batch window processing is to be done than there is adequate time for, the design of the application must be altered. One of the complications of batch window estimation is that ad hoc reporting requirements can vary widely from night to night.

General Performance Considerations

Assuming that the discipline exists to create and maintain a DB2 production online environment, there are nevertheless upper limits of performance beyond which DB2 cannot perform. (Every piece of online software has an upper limit, commonly referred to as the *maximum transaction arrival rate,* or MTAR). On a large processor such as a 3090-400, DB2 under Release 2 can run up to 45 transactions per second, assuming that the discipline exists to create a production online environment.

If the production online environment is not created and maintained with discipline, then the MTAR for DB2 drops substantially. The production environment is the environment in which the day-to-day transactions of the enterprise are run. The production environment is typified by the management of primitive data in a highly structured manner. Under normal conditions unstructured processing, such as that found in the ad hoc reporting environment, is not considered to be production.

The peak-period arrival rate must be carefully estimated by the designer (in conjunction with the data base administrator and system administrator) prior to the selection of DB2 as the DBMS of choice. If the peak-period processing rate exceeds the MTAR for DB2, then other high-performance software, such as IMS Fast Path or TPF, should be chosen for the application.

Peak-period processing is really a system parameter, not an application parameter. For example, if an application designer estimates a peak-period arrival rate for his or her application of 25 transactions per second, then DB2 will comfortably handle the workload. If the application is to be run on a system that is already experiencing 30 transactions per second at peak period, then DB2 may be eliminated as the DBMS of choice, or the application designer must find a less heavily loaded processor.

Peak-period activity estimation can be difficult. Some of the techniques for the estimation of the peak-period activity include

- historical comparisons: what other systems have done in relation to the needs of the application to be built
- analytical modeling: using software packages to simulate a typical day's activity
- paper and pencil estimates: using common sense and crude measurements to "guesstimate" peak-period requirements

Unfortunately, each of these techniques has many pitfalls. For example, a concentrated focus on the technical environment and technical requirements may well yield a good understanding of the details of the technical needs, but the ultimate results achieved will be meaningless unless business needs are factored into the estimates as well. If the efficiency and polish of the new system will attract 50 percent more customers, then the marginal workload required to handle the new customers must be factored into peak-period resource requirements estimates. Focusing on technology and not on the business aspects can lead to grossly incorrect results.

Summary

The first step in the establishment of the online production environment is to clearly outline what features and facilities of DB2 are to be used and what features and facilities are not to be used. The rigor demanded of the online environment to achieve good, consistent online performance is such that not all DB2 options are applicable.

The basis for performance in DB2 is the minimization of I/O. I/O consumption can be reduced (in some cases) by an awareness of the physical structures of DB2, the usage of data clustering, and the establishment and usage of table relationships.

Some of the specific limitations of the online production environment are

- no QMF processing
- limited DXT processing
- online access of data through standard TP monitors
- the execution of only designed transactions
- no data base structure changes during the online day
- execution of precompiled SQL only
- usage of limited views of data
- no sorting, summing, averaging, or the like
- no utility execution during the online day

CHAPTER 2

DATA BASE DESIGN
FOR DB2

Once the production online environment is established, good, consistent performance on a systemwide basis can become a reality. The next step in the achievement of good online performance is the translation of user requirements into a design that yields good performance. The two facets in the design of high performance systems are data base design and transaction design. Both facets of design are equally necessary to achieve optimal online performance.

CONCEPTUAL DATA BASE DESIGN

Most of the considerations of performance in data base design occur during physical design. Consequently, this chapter discusses data base design at the physical level almost to the exclusion of other aspects of design.

Prior to physical data base design, the conceptual foundation for data base design (which includes data modeling, entity-relationship analysis, and data item set derivation) should be laid, for many reasons, among them performance. For a detailed explanation of conceptual data base design, refer to my *Information Systems Architecture* and *Information Engineering for the Practitioner* (see references at the end of this book).

The conceptual design activities that precede the physical data base design should have accomplished (at the least!)

- the consolidation of identical or similar data across broad functional areas
- the separation of primitive and derived data
- the organization of primitive data into major subject areas
- the definition of the interface between data and processes
- the recognition of commonality and the preservation of uniqueness of data and processing
- the definition of keys and foreign keys throughout the data structures
- the definition of the boundaries or limitations of the data model and the resulting data bases
- specific data characteristics, such as data definitions, data values, data representations, and encoding.

FROM A CONCEPTUAL MODEL TO A PHYSICAL DESIGN

After the conceptual design is complete, the next design step is to use the conceptual design as input into physical design activities. Some activities of this intermediate step include

- identification of the number of occurrences of data
- identification of the volatility and growth of data
- identification of the system response time requirements
- estimation of the projected transaction workload, both in total and during peak-period processing

```
date employee attended school             :   :   :   :
school attended                           :   :   :   :
degree sought                          date of pay(n)
major                                  net pay
social security number                 number of dependents
employee number                        married/single?
cumulative FICA paid                   special deductions amount(1)
cumulative annual pay                  special deductions amount(2)
cumulative annual state tax            special deductions amount(3)
cumulative annual Federal tax          special deductions amount(4)
date of hire                           limits of deductibility(1)
location of hire                       limits of deductibility(2)
dependent(1) identification            limits of deductibility(3)
dependent(2) identification            limits of deductibility(4)
dependent(3) identification            FICA per pay period
dependent(4) identification            state tax per pay period
dependent(1) relationship              Federal tax per pay period
dependent(2) relationship              insurer number
dependent(3) relationship              liability limits
dependent(4) relationship              date of insurance coverage
date of pay(1)                         accident coverage amount
date of pay(2)                         illness coverage amount
date of pay(3)                         death coverage amount
```

Figure 2.1 Unnormalized data elements.

- estimation of the amount of overnight batch processing to be done, both on the average and at peak periods
- identification of annual or monthly periods of peak processing
- creation-migration-conversion plan formulation
- identification of system availability requirements

Once conceptual data base design has been done and the transformation to the physical form of data has been undertaken, the design of the details of the physical data base (with an emphasis on performance) can commence.

NORMALIZED DATA STRUCTURES

Before the designer of a DB2 data base begins to think about the technical details of specification of a physical data base, a more strategic issue of data base design must be considered.

The relational model of data, on which DB2 is based, calls for elements of data to be grouped together so that individual elements of data directly depend on their key for their existence. In other words, if the key of the data for a specific

```
date employee attended school         net pay
school attended                        number of dependents
degree sought                          married/single?
major                                  special deductions amount
social security number                 limits of deductibility
employee number                        FICA per pay period
cumulative FICA paid                   state tax per pay period
cumulative annual pay                  Federal tax per pay period
cumulative annual state tax            insurer number
cumulative annual Federal tax          liability limits
date of hire                           date of insurance coverage
location of hire                       accident coverage amount
dependent identification               illness coverage amount
dependent relationship                 death coverage amount
date of pay
```

Figure 2.2 Normalized data elements—first normal form.

Employee Number
Date of Hire
Location of Hire

(dependent relationship)
Dependent's Id
Dependent's Relationship

(pay relationship)
Cumulative FICA
Cumulative Pay
Cumulative State Tax
Cumulative Federal Tax

(education relationship)
School
Degree
Date Attended

(pay history relationship)
Pay Date
Net Pay
FICA Paid
State Tax Paid
Federal Tax Paid

(insurance relationship)
Insurer Number
Liability Limits
Date of Coverage
Accident Coverage
Illness Coverage
Death Coverage

(deduction relationship)
Number Dependents
Married/Single?
Special Deduction Amounts
Limits of Deductibility

Figure 2.3 Normalized data
elements—Second normal form.

occurrence of data does not exist, then the dependent data elements do not exist. This brief and untechnical explanation of normalization is best illustrated in terms of an example. Suppose the data base designer is to structure the data found in Figure 2.1.

From the unnormalized set of data elements, a set of normalized data elements are created—in the case shown, normalized to the first normal form. The first level of normalization is shown with repeating groups removed in Figure 2.2.

The next level of normalization is achieved by grouping data in accordance with the direct existence of the data, as shown in Figure 2.3.

The next level of normalization is achieved by recognizing indirect dependencies of data, as shown by Figure 2.4.

In the grouping of data found in Figure 2.4, any given data element will not exist if the key for the element does not exist. For example, in the employee base table, if employee number 123 exists, then employee 123 will have a date of hire and a location of hire, but if employee 123 does not exist (or never has existed), then there will be no date of hire or location of hire for employee 123.

Figure 2.4 shows the logical grouping of data according to the rules of

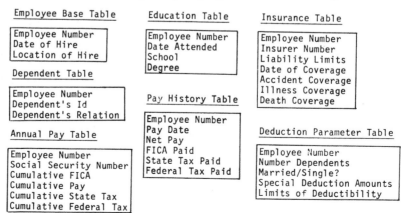

Figure 2.4 Data elements that have been normalized and organized into tables.

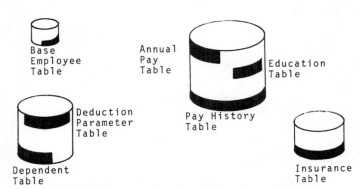

Figure 2.5 The physical spread of data when normalized tables are directly translated into physical data bases.

normalization. The questions then become, What if each of these normalized tables is turned into its own relational table? If each of the relational tables is turned into its own physical data base, as is certainly technically feasible, what are the implications? The result of literally translating normalized data into physical data base design is shown by Figure 2.5.

Figure 2.5 shows that when each of the tables is used as a basis for physical data base design, those data tend to be spread across many physical locations. As long as there is no need to interrelate the data from one table to the next on a frequent basis, then there is no problem. When data from one table need to be related to data from another table (or tables) on a frequent basis, however, the result is much I/O, as each interconnection of data from one data base to the next requires a physical I/O (unless, of course, there is a fortuitous connection of data made in the buffer area). Figure 2.6 shows the connectivity of data across tables and the resulting I/O.

Figure 2.6 shows the I/O that must be done for each employee to satisfy simple payroll processing. From a performance perspective, the spread of data across different locations introduces much I/O.

A more efficient structuring of data would be to consolidate some of the tables shown in Figure 2.5 into a single table, even though the consolidation violates the rules of normalization. Figure 2.7 suggests one way that the data may be combined to enhance performance.

Figure 2.7 shows that three normalized tables of data have been combined into one. Because of the aggregation, the data will be stored in a single location on DASD. Upon accessing the data for any employee, *all* the data that are stored in the location will be available in the same I/O. The net result of storing unnormalized data together is the reduced need for I/O. The net effect of reducing the I/O required by a system is the enhancement of performance. Of course, when data

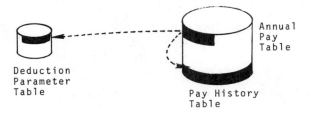

Figure 2.6 I/O must be done to three separate locations when a program wants to use a foreign key to relate data.

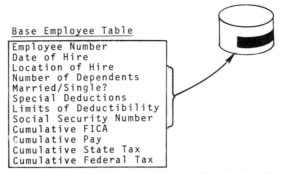

Base Employee Table

```
Employee Number
Date of Hire
Location of Hire
Number of Dependents
Married/Single?
Special Deductions
Limits of Deductibility
Social Security Number
Cumulative FICA
Cumulative Pay
Cumulative State Tax
Cumulative Federal Tax
```

Figure 2.7 By grouping base data into a common table with deduction data and annual pay data, the designer has short-circuited the need for I/O that would otherwise be needed to make intertable connections if data were separated into tables in a normalized form.

are denormalized, they should be denormalized to optimize the most frequently executed processes.

The designer should look at all the processes to be executed in the production environment and select the most frequently executed processes for analysis. Then the designer should denormalize the data to suit the needs of the most frequently run processes. The remaining processes that do not have data physically optimized for their execution will have to pay the penalty of I/O for the dynamic interconnectability of relational data.

Denormalization of data can be carried too far. All the data in Figure 2.5 can be arranged into a single table and into a single data base. However, if denormalization is carried to that extreme, another performance factor arises, that of the locking of data and the probability of contention. When data are neatly tucked into small, highly fragmented data bases, there is little chance that two or more users will wish to access or update the same data at the same time. When many data are conglomerated together, as happens in an extreme case of denormalization, however, then the odds are greatly improved that two or more users wish to access or update the same data at the same time, thus introducing a negative performance factor.

INDEXING DATA

One of the biggest performance considerations of DB2 is selecting fields for indexing. The issue of indexing fields has two facets. In accessing data, indexes can greatly reduce I/O requirements, but in the change and update of data, indexes can cost I/O. The issue, then, of creating, maintaining, and using indexes is one of trade-off between data access and data update.

To illustrate the potential I/O savings of an index, consider the simple relational table shown in Figure 2.8.

Figure 2.8 shows a table that contains an employee's educational history. Consider the I/O required to service the request to find all employees who attended Arizona University.

Employee Number	Date Attended	School	Degree	Major
1456	1967	Yale	--	Math
1456	1970	Arizona	BS	Math
1456	1972	Arizona	MS	Com Sci
1459	1981	Miami	BS	Business
⋮	⋮	⋮	⋮	⋮

Page 1

Employee Number	Date Attended	School	Degree	Major
1701	1968	UCLA	BS	Civ Eng
1714	1979	Harvard	BS	English
1714	1984	U Texas	PhD	English
1743	1980	U Colo	BS	Anthro
1752	1963	Boston Coll	BA	Spanish
⋮	⋮	⋮	⋮	⋮

Page 2

Figure 2.8 An employee education table whose primary key is employee date of attendance.

```
SELECT EMPLOYEE
FROM EMPTAB
WHERE SCHOOL = 'ARIZ'
```

This request against an unindexed employee's data requires that all rows in all pages be queried. In short, if there are n pages, then n I/Os will be required to service the request.

But suppose the table in Figure 2.8 were indexed for each employee on school attended, as shown in Figure 2.9.

Figure 2.9 shows that with the index (which is highly condensed into a few blocks of data), the query of which employees went to Arizona University is easily answered. The school attended index is accessed and based upon the information found in the index, only those pages and rows that are appropriate are physically accessed. In short, instead of accessing all pages and randomly searching for data that fits the criteria, the index allows data to be precisely and directly accessed, thus greatly economizing on the I/Os required to satisfy a request.

But indexes can save I/O in other ways. Suppose the end user wished not to see the names of the employees that went to Arizona University but wished merely for a count of the employees that had attended Arizona University, as per the request

```
SELECT COUNT(*)
FROM EMPTAB
WHERE SCHOOL = 'ARIZ'
```

In this case the query can be satisfied entirely in the index without having to access the primary data. Much I/O is saved by satisfying this request in the index.

As useful as indexes are in the saving of I/O in the access of data, indexes have a corresponding cost as the data that is indexed changes and needs to be updated. Consider the simple table in Figure 2.10.

Employee Education Table

	Employee Number	Date Attended	School	Degree	Major
Page 1	1456	1967	Yale	--	Math
	1456	1970	Arizona	BS	Math
	1456	1972	Arizona	MS	Com Sci
	1459	1981	Miami	BS	Business
	:	:	:	:	:
Page 2	1701	1968	UCLA	BS	Civ Eng
	1714	1979	Harvard	BS	English
	1714	1984	U Texas	PhD	English
	1743	1980	U Colo	BS	Anthro
	1752	1963	Boston Coll	BA	Spanish
	:	:	:	:	:

School Index

```
Ariz    Ariz    Ariz    Ariz    ArizSt  ArizSt ..........
page1   page1   page4   page10  page6   page8  ..........
entry1  entry2  entry2  entry6  entry4  entry6 ..........


Harv    Harv    Hofstr  Hofstr  IllSt   IllSt  ..........
page10  page2   page29  page81  page17  page6  ..........
entry4  entry2  entry2  entry3  entry7  entry8 ..........
```

Figure 2.9 An index on school allows the employee education table to be accessed directly based on the value of the school that the employee attended.

The table in Figure 2.10 shows the department in which an employee works. There is a department index that shows the department of an employee.

Consider the I/O that occurs when an employee changes departments. One I/O must be done to update the primary table, and another I/O must be done to delete the index reference from the old department. Still another I/O must be done to the index to insert the reference to the employee's new department. In all, three I/Os were required to accommodate the change of departments. If there were no index by department, only one I/O would have been needed to accommodate the

Employee Number	Department
1456	43J
1607	14BR
1995	QA1
0121	43J
:	:

Department/Employee Index

Dept	Employee Number	Page	Entry
001A	0081	109	9
001A	0094	029	1
001A	0189	208	13
001A	0971	018	4
:	:	:	:

Figure 2.10 A table showing the department in which an employee works and an index on the employees in a department.

change in data. In general, when data that is indexed undergo change, two I/Os per index are required to keep the data current.

Another consideration of indexes concerns indexing on data values that occur frequently. For example, in a personnel file employees may be classified as exempt or nonexempt (having a field content of E or N). Creating an index on a commonly occurring value such as exempt or nonexempt is probably wasteful. When searches based on the value need to be done, actually accessing each page row by row is most likely faster than accessing the data on an index.

The designer must constantly be aware of the I/O requirements at update, creation, and deletion time, which are traded off for access efficiency.

REFERENTIAL INTEGRITY

Referential integrity is the capability of a system to keep the relationships between two occurrences of data synchronized in the face of change when data are interrelated by means of a foreign key. DB2 Release 2 depends upon the application programmer to implement and maintain referential integrity. DB2, of course, uses foreign keys to relate different tables together as shown in Figure 2.11.

Figure 2.11 shows three DB2 tables: a parts table, a supplier table, and a supplier-part cross-reference table. Consider what happens when part number

Part Number	Amount	Descriptor	U/M
1987ty-9	560	Manifold	Unit
776t-908	10700	Base Plate	Tub
66509-u	56	Housing Mold	Unit
10087-pw	600900	Bearings	Tub
9978-rtw12	6700	Platform Assem	Tray
⋮	⋮	⋮	⋮

Supplier	Address	Contact	Phone
Jones Hdware	123 Main, Dallas	J Cash	555-1212
Emporium	90 Broad, Atlanta	J Carter	679-5142
Wilson St	13 First, Miami	R Acuff	998-0013
Pace Whse	1 S Jstreet, Denver	R Clark	077-5519
⋮	⋮	⋮	⋮

Supplier/Part	Number
Jones Hdware	10087-pw
Jones Hdware	66509-u
Jones Hdware	887-yt65
Jones Hdware	9987-trqe
Pace Whse	776t-908
Pace Whse	880-887rq
⋮	⋮

Figure 2.11 Three relational tables: a parts table, a supplier table, and a cross-reference table from supplier to part.

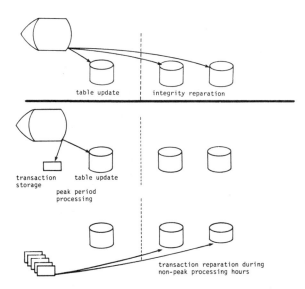

Figure 2.12 (*a*). Option 1—foreign key reparation during peak processing hours, normally done at the expense of performance; (*b*). Option 2—storing transactions that update, delete, or create foreign keys in a queue and repairing data base integrity during off-peak hours. This option leaves the data bases unsynchronized for a period of time, but enhances performance during peak-period processing.

10087-pw is deleted from the parts table. For the system to remain "pure," all references to part number 10087-pw must be immediately deleted in all the tables that reference part numbers. In the example shown, the supplier-parts cross-reference would need to have the Jones Hardware reference for that part deleted. If the cross-reference is not deleted, then the cross-reference will show that Jones Hardware is the supplier of a nonexistent part.

From a performance perspective, there are several options in the management of referential integrity. One option is to delete all references to a part when the part is deleted as an integral part of the online transaction. Although this might require much I/O in the middle of the online day, thus causing a major performance difficulty, repairing the logical inconsistency on the spot keeps the data of the system pure.

If absolute purity (that is, up to the second accuracy) is not required, then another strategy is to wait until the peak hours of processing have passed and then repair the inconsistency in the data base. The transaction that has deleted the part keeps track of the fact that it has executed successfully and is stored with other transactions that have likewise executed successfully. Then, during nonpeak hours, those transactions are batched together and run against the tables that relate to data bases that have been updated during peak-hour processing. Figure 2.12 illustrates these two options.

MULTIPLE OCCURRENCES OF DATA

Data managed by a DBMS normally occur many times. For example, a customer table may have 100,000 rows, and a parts table may have 10,000 parts. Such are the economies of handling data under a DBMS. However, data occasionally occurs in large enough numbers that special design techniques are required. For

Customer Number	Date	Activity Number	Activity Type	Amount	Location
3341-0	Jun1286	000001	DDA	136.90	AZS
3341-0	Jun1286	000002	DDA	1080.87	AZS
3341-0	Jun2386	000001	DDA	73.97	AZS
3341-0	Jun2486	000001	DDA	25.00	AZS
3981-8	Jun1186	000001	DDA	760.00	FRW
3981-8	Jun1586	000001	L--	1000.00	HGA
⋮	⋮	⋮	⋮	⋮	⋮

Figure 2.13 A simple design for the table for the banking activities of the customers of a bank.

example, suppose a bank has 100,000 customers and suppose each customer has, on the average, 25 banking activities each month. Now suppose the bank wishes to store 5 years of history per customer in a DB2 data base. The number of rows to be stored, then, is

$$100,000 \times 25 \times 12 \times 5 = 150,000,000 \text{ rows}$$

The question arises, Is all the data that will be held in the data base necessary? An interesting analysis can be made of the probability of access of data. Of the 150,000,000 rows of data stored, how many will ever be used, and what is the cost of the storage? The first issue that must be settled is whether the cost of storage is effective from a business perspective. One approach would be to create one row for each customer activity, as shown by the data base design in Figure 2.13.

A word of explanation is in order for this table. The key is customer number, date, and activity number. Activity number is required to force uniqueness of the key. Without activity number, any customer doing more than one activity on the same day would create nonunique keys. Although this approach to data base design is simple, it carries with it some problems that can hamper system performance and availability. If the data is nonclustered and there is one index entry for each row, 150,000,000 index entries are required. Moreover, what about the number of index entries that will be required for indexing on nonkey fields?

Consider the work required of the system when the definition of a given field needs to be modified. The new definition of the data must be presented to the system. Then the field must be unloaded in its old format and reloaded in its new format. If the field has an index, the index must be recreated. In short, the volume of data to be manipulated in the redefinition of data presents its own special problems that are brought about solely by the existence of the volume of data.

Now consider what would happen if common usage of the data dictated that several day's banking activities for a customer needed to be accessed, as illustrated by the following request: For customer 1234, retrieve all banking activity for the week of July 20 to July 26, 1986. Locating the index records does not require a large amount of I/O because the index is tightly packed and contains several levels. What about the I/O required to access the rows of data? The first row is in page 99, the next row is in page 32, the next in page 45, and so forth; in other words, even though the index is compactly arranged and efficient to traverse in terms of I/O consumption, the data pointed to by the index is widely dispersed

Customer Number	Year/ Month	Location	Group	1st Day	Amt	2nd Day	Amt	3rd Day	Amt	4th Day	Amt	5th Day	Amt
3341-0	Jun86	AZS	00001	12	136.90	12	1080.87	23	73.97	24	25.00	--	----
3981-8	Jun86	FRW	00001	11	760.00	14	458.00	14	12.50	15	100.00	16	167.98
3981-8	Jun86	FRW	00002	18	90.00	19	15.00	21	100.00	22	35.00	23	5.00
3981-8	JUN86	HGA	00001	15	1000.00	--	----	--	----	--	----	--	----
:	:	:	:	:	:	:	:	:	:	:	:	:	:

Figure 2.14 A different arrangement of customer activity data that packs the data into the table more tightly. The effectiveness of this approach depends on a knowledge about the customers' data and the ability of the data base to be tailored.

and requires much I/O for its access. As long as the rows are not clustered, going from one row to the next requires one I/O per row because each row is in a physically different page, and for a significant number of rows, the I/O consumed mounts quickly.

Now suppose the rows were clustered. This means that going from one row to the next does not require I/O unless a new page is encountered. In addition, there are fewer index entries for the index pointing to the primary key. So, clustering of data is the first step toward managing a large amount of data.

Other design options can also be utilized. One such option is depicted by Figure 2.14.

Several features of the design in Figure 2.14 enhance performance. The primary key of the table is customer number, year and month of activity, location, and group number. Following the key are up to five occurrences of data showing actual date of the month of the activity and the amount of the activity. When there are fewer than five occurrences of activities of the same key, null values are used. When there are more than five activities for the key, then a new group of activities is created, thus building a new row with a unique key.

Some of the efficiencies of this structuring of data are

- many fewer index entries, regardless of whether the rows are clustered or not. Roughly, a fourth of the index entries will be needed in the example shown.

- data are compacted. Redundant occurrences of data, such as month and year, have been eliminated.

- once a row is in the buffer, all five occurrences of data will be accessible in every case.

The effectiveness of the design depends greatly on the knowledge of customers' habits. For example, if customers frequent many different locations to execute banking activities, then this structuring of data may actually cost performance and space, but as long as customers are creatures of habit and have their own favorite tellers or ATMs, then the structuring of data as depicted saves space and I/O.

The selection of the number occurrences that should fit into any row is not a random selection. The number of occurrences (in the case of the example shown in Figure 2.14) depends upon

- the physical block size into which the row must fit
- the number of occurrences of data, the average, and the standard deviation
- the pattern of access of data, that is, whether it is random, sequential, or whatever

- the pattern of insertions and deletions
- the inability to index an occurrence directly once the occurrence has entered a row

The designer then has available a number of options in the management of large numbers of rows.

When there is a large quantity of data, oftentimes it makes sense to organize data into collections that are active or inactive (that is, archived). An active data base is one that contains data with a high probability of access. An archival data base is one that contains data with a low probability of access, usually nonrecent historical data. By separating the two types of data during design, the designer circumvents many problems during implementation.

One technique for the management of active and archival data is the placement of active data on the fastest storage device available and the placement of archival data on slower storage devices. In such a manner the hierarchy of storage is matched with the usage of data.

One useful criterion for determining when data should be archived is whether it makes sense to update the data. Generally speaking, data with the potential to be updated should not be archived and data that do not need to be updated may be archived. This division of data fits ingeniously with the data management technology found in both the operational and archival environments because operational technology is geared for update and archival technology is not.

For a large collection of data, it is not unusual to have 5 percent of the data in the active data base and 95 percent of the data in the archival data base. The separation of data makes set-at-a-time processing of data viable.

As an example, suppose an insurance company wishes to create a five-year claim history file. One approach is simply to create a single large data base. Another approach is to analyze what data will be needed the most. The active data base will typically be made up of the claims of the last three months, all claims over $50,000, and all claims of selected clients. All other claims are shuffled off to the archival files. On a periodic basis, active data older than three months is sent to the archival file.

In the archiving of data where data is stored in separate locations, a useful technique in some cases is to create an I/O module that knows the location of data. In such a manner, the actual location is masked from the programmer.

However, separating large amounts of data according to archival needs is only one way to break up large collections of data. There are many other criteria that can be used for separation. Some of them are

- separation by function. Instead of a parts data base that contains many rows, several data bases can be formed, each of which is smaller than the collective data base, but which, taken together, logically comprise the large collection of data. A drive train data base, a body data base, an interior data base, a steering data base, and so on can be created so that all of the assembly is represented in the different tables.
- separation by key range. Suppose a parts data base needs to be physically subdivided into smaller tables. One table contains parts whose key begins

with zero, the next table contains keys whose first digit is one, and so forth. This way a large data base can arbitrarily be split into multiple data bases.

- separation by date. Suppose an archival data base is to be created. The archived data can be separated by year, by year and month, by year, month, and day, and so forth. The granularity of the split depends on the amount of data and the usage of data.

- separation by geographical division. A retail consumer vendor can have either a single, large customer data base or several smaller data bases that segment the customers according to geographic location. The retailer may have, for example, a Northern California data base, a Southern California data base, a Central California data base, and so on.

- separation by customer classification. A bank can have a single accounts data base, or the bank may choose to have the accounts broken up by customer classification, such as commercial accounts, individual accounts (active), individual accounts (inactive), and individual accounts (upscale).

The data base designer can segment large collections of data in many different ways. Given the set processing orientation of DB2, the segmentation has many advantages.

Guidelines for the designer in the selection of the proper criteria for separation include

- are the categories chosen for separation mutually exclusive? If not, more than one occurrence of data may fit in multiple categories. (If an occurrence of data fits in more than one category, then the integrity of duplicate data must be maintained at the application level, something normally not desired.)

- will the categorization effectively reduce the size of the data bases? On occasion subcategorization appears to reduce the size of the data bases, but an analysis at the physical level shows that only a small reduction is being achieved. When the bulk of data is not reduced by subcategorization, nearly all data fits into a single subcategory.

- will the subcategorization of one data base fit with the subcategorization criteria of another data base? For example, if in an insurance company all customers are subdivided by geographic region, it may be difficult to subdivide all accounts by another criteria, such as upscale, commercial, and active customers.

VARIABLE LENGTH FIELDS

One option the data base designer has with DB2 is that of variable length fields. The proper design and use of variable length fields is important to performance because the improper use of variable length fields can lead to unnecessary I/O. In addition, the management of variable length fields requires a certain amount of CPU overhead. Another cost incurred in the usage of variable length fields is the overhead of storage required for each variable field. Two bytes of storage are required to identify the existence and length of the variable field.

A variable length field is one that can have different lengths for different occurrences of data. Names and text are common candidates for variable length fields. As a simple example, suppose the designer has specified NAME as a field in a table. Then JEANNE FRIEDMAN will require 15 bytes of information for its occurrence as a variable length field and TF CHANG will require 8 bytes of information for its occurrence as a variable length field.

There is nothing wrong with variable length fields per se, as far as performance is concerned, but instances can arise where variable length fields can cause much CPU and I/O to be consumed. For example, JEANNE FRIEDMAN exists in a table as an occurrence of a variable length field. Jeanne Friedman marries and decides to take the name of her husband. The programmer retrieves JEANNE FRIEDMAN and wishes to replace that name with JEANNE SYL-VESTER. So far no unnecessary amount of I/O has been expended, but trying to replace 16 bytes where once there were 15 presents an opportunity for I/O. I/O is used when the extra byte cannot be accommodated by available free space in the page upon replacement.

If the data is loosely packed (that is, packed with much free space) probably no data management is required. If the data is tightly packed, however, at the very least the row containing JEANNE SYLVESTER must be replaced within the page. If there is no room for the new row in the page, another page where there is available space must be located. Locating that page and adjusting the index does require I/O.

The converse design problem—that of replacing smaller variable length fields than what was originally retrieved—does not cost I/O but does cost space in the data base that cannot be easily retrieved. For example, suppose Jeanne Friedman had married Fred Smith and decided to change her name. To reclaim the space under normal circumstances requires a data base reorganization. For all practical purposes, the DB2 page has lost three bytes of data until the next reorganization.

One caution is that variable length fields can cost I/O or wasted space when variable length fields, once created, are allowed to be updated. Of course, if the length of the field is established at the moment of creation of the row and never changes, then there is no performance conflict. For example, suppose a title company wishes to list the street address of each property it manages, along with other information about the property. Once the street address is written, the chance that the address will ever change is highly unlikely. But, the amount of storage used for one property description and another differs dramatically, so a variable field definition is in order. The stability of the description is such that the row of data, once created, is very unlikely to change, thus minimizing the problems with I/O or wasted space.

The DB2 physical data base design option PCTFREE can be used to alleviate some of the problems of variable length rows. PCTFREE is used in the loading of a table and indicates the amount of free space (in terms of percentages) that is to be left unused after the loading of the first record. If the designer

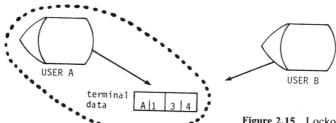

Figure 2.15 Lockout occurs when user A and user B are attempting to access and update the terminal security data base at the same time.

anticipates variable rows with a high degree of volatility, then free space can be left. If the space becomes used or otherwise unavailable, however, a reorganization of the data must be done to reallocate free space. Note that FREEPAGE, another related DB2 physical data base design option, does nothing to alleviate the problems of variable rows flowing beyond the boundary of a single page when the size of a variable length field changes.

CONTROL DATA BASES

Although most relational tables contain data such as customers, accounts, or part numbers that are directly related to an application, data that can be considered auxiliary (or utilitarian) are frequently useful in a relational table as well. Such data bases can be called *control data bases* and typically hold security data, audit data, table data, terminal data, and the like. There is nothing wrong with control data bases per se, but they are often candidates for performance bottlenecks.

One of the online features of DB2 is locking of data. Locking prevents two online users from accessing and updating the same data at the same time. Locking in DB2 normally occurs at two levels: the page level and the tablespace level. Furthermore, locking can be exclusive or shared. When locking is *exclusive*, no other program can access the data while the data is locked. When locking is *shared*, read-only access of the data is allowed while the data is locked.

Figure 2.15 shows that user A has accessed and is updating (or at least has the potential for updating) a terminal security table. In the example shown, locking is exclusive and at the page level.

While user A is controlling the terminal security data base, user B must wait. The two users are in contention for the same data at the same time, and the system

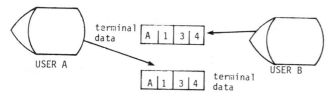

Figure 2.16 One solution to the problem of lockout is to duplicate the data if the application will allow.

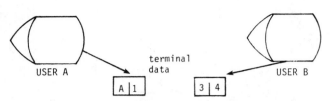

Figure 2.17 Separating data at the design level is another solution to the problems posed by lockout.

is essentially single-threaded. User A must free the terminal security data for user B to be able to continue processing.

There are several solutions at the design level to the problems presented by control data bases, depending upon the needs of the application.

One solution is to duplicate the data in the terminal security data base, as shown by Figure 2.16. In this case, when user A wishes to access and update the terminal security data, there is no contention with user B because user B is accessing a copy of the data that is being held by user A, not the actual data being held by user A. This solution depends upon the fact that the terminal security data can be duplicated, which is often not the case.

Another option is to subdivide the terminal security data base into small units of access and physically separate the data (that is, creating physically separate tables or separating different types of data into separate tables), as shown in Figure 2.17.

In Figure 2.17, there is no contention between users A and B because the users are after different parts of the terminal security data base. The design techniques of separation and replication can also be used for other data bases where contention and locking are potential problems.

The techniques discussed for the management of control data bases have their downside. Duplicating data and breaking data down into very fine divisions have implications for integrity, update, program development and maintenance, and other matters.

Data Views

One feature of DB2 is data views. A *view* is nothing more than a logical perspective of data, as opposed to a physical perspective of data. Figure 2.18 shows a typical DB2 view of account data and activity.

Views can be useful for creating distinct, easily perceived perspectives of data. From a performance standpoint, however, views can be harmful to performance when the background work done by the system is factored into the view. When a view spans two or more tables, a large amount of I/O may be required to service the view. On one hand, the view appears as a simple structuring of data to the user. On the other hand, the view may require large amounts of I/O. As a result, the designer should be careful in the assignment and usage of views. Generally speaking, the designer is safest with presenting data as it is defined in its table.

When views do not span multiple tables, they may actually enhance performance. Consider the table shown in Figure 2.19.

Suppose the account, date opened, and location fields were indexed, and the remaining fields in the table were not. The view allows the user to access the table

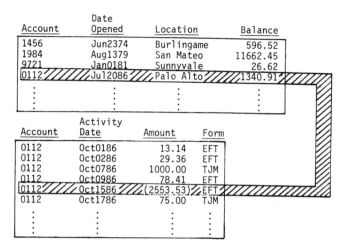

Account	Date Opened	Location	Balance
1456	Jun2374	Burlingame	596.52
1984	Aug1379	San Mateo	11662.45
9721	Jan0181	Sunnyvale	26.62
0112	Jul2086	Palo Alto	1340.91

Account	Activity Date	Amount	Form
0112	Oct0186	13.14	EFT
0112	Oct0286	29.36	EFT
0112	Oct0786	1000.00	TJM
0112	Oct0986	78.41	EFT
0112	Oct1586	(2553.53)	EFT
0112	Oct1786	75.00	TJM

Figure 2.18 A view of data: the account information and the activity for October 15 for account 0112. The view spans two tables.

only on fields that are quickly and efficiently retrievable (other than indexing on balance, which is in any case a questionable field for indexing). Because a subset of data is chosen that does not span multiple tables and that does not allow access or retrieval on nonindexed fields, a view may actually enhance performance.

SEQUENTIALLY ACCESSING DB2 DATA

DB2 data can be accessed either sequentially or randomly. If only a small amount of data is to be handled, the issue of the basic access path is not terribly important. In the face of large amounts of data, however, the designer must carefully choose the basic access path because much I/O can be wasted if the designer fails to make the correct choice.

The first method of organizing DB2 data is in an unclustered fashion, as shown by Figure 2.20.

The index in Figure 2.20 is sequenced and points to data, which is itself randomly organized. Unclustered data is ideal for online transaction processing that must access a single row of data at a time, satisfying such online activity as "What is the quantity on hand of part 20156?"

If more than one row of data is required (especially if many rows of data are required), then accessing DB2 unclustered data may cost many I/Os, as the satisfaction of one row request through the index to the next may cause an I/O for each row requested.

A second design option is to cluster data, so that as many row requests in one page can be satisfied as possible. In other words, when data is clustered, an

Account	Opened	Location	Balance	Options	Unique Identification
1456	Jun2374	Burlingame	586.52	AQR	1585
1984	Aug1379	San Mateo	11662.46	---	JV72
9721	Jan0181	Sunnyvale	26.62	ARM	3081
0112	Jul2086	Palo Alto	137.78	AD	4381

Figure 2.19 A view of data looking at a subset of a table.

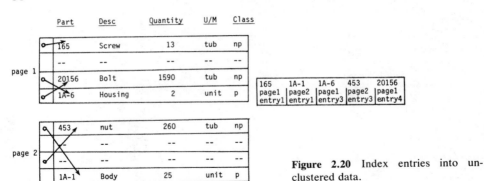

Figure 2.20 Index entries into un-clustered data.

I/O is done to retrieve a row, but to retrieve the next row, and the next, and so on, no more I/Os are needed as long as the rows are in the same page and the page is being held in the buffer area. If rows are arranged in a sequence meaningful to the application processing, a minimal amount of I/O is needed. Consider the data in Figure 2.21.

Suppose the application designer desires to go from one part number to the next in sequence. Retrieving part 165 requires an I/O, but no I/O is required for the retrieval of parts 1A-1, 1A-6, and 453 because the page is already resident in the buffer area and doesn't require another I/O. Only when part 20156 is fetched will another I/O be required.

If clustering of data can save I/O upon access, shouldn't all tables be clustered? The answer is no because upon insertion of data, clustering of data can actually cost I/O. For example, suppose the row of the part number 1A-5 were to be inserted into the small data base shown in Figure 2.21. The row must be inserted into the middle of the page, but there is no room for it. As a consequence, part of the data in the page must be moved to other pages, and the consequence is more I/O required for data management. Clustering of data has other disadvantages as well.

Consider the I/O required if the part table is to be accessed by means of description. Assume an index is built on DESCRIPTION, as shown by Figure 2.22.

If the parts are accessed in order of description, the effect in terms of I/O consumed is the same as if the parts were unclustered.

Clustering, then, can be used to optimally arrange data in a physical sequence that is propitious for sequential access. However, only one physical

Figure 2.21 Index entries into clustered data.

Part	Desc	Quantity	U/M	Class
165	Screw	13	tub	np
1A-1	Body	25	unit	p
1A-6	Housing	2	unit	p
453	Nut	260	tub	np

page 1

Part	Desc	Quantity	U/M	Class
20156	Bolt	1590	tub	np
--	--	--	--	--
--	--	--	--	--
--	--	--	--	--

page 2

165 pagel entry1	1A-1 pagel entry2	1A-6 pagel entry3	453 pagel entry4	21056 page2 entry1

Body pagel entry1	Bolt page2 entry1	Housing pagel entry3	Nut pagel entry4	Screw pagel entry1

Figure 2.22 (a). Index entries into clustered data; (b). Index entries into a clustered table on other than the primary key.

optimization of data is possible, even though the data may be sequentially accessed any number of ways. It is a temptation to say that an index can be used to sequentially reorder data in a manner other than that used for the clustering of the data.

If *all* the application requires is to see the key values of the index in another order, then an index can, in fact, be used to resequence clustered data. If more than the key values (or the data that is stored in every index entry) is required to satisfy the query and access of data, then using an index to resequence data is terribly wasteful of I/O, as the I/O required to go from each index entry into the data area can be enormous.

As a consequence, if large amounts of data need to be accessed in a sequence other than the order in which they are clustered and if there is a need to see more than the mere key value of the data, then it is usually less expensive (in terms of I/O consumed) to enter the data base, strip off appropriate records, sort the records, and create a new table. Figure 2.23 shows two typical stripping techniques.

In Figure 2.23, one algorithm strips the clustered data on part and description data, but does so for all the records. The other algorithm strips all types of data for a certain classification of data. In either case, the resulting data can be sorted and tightly packed so that efficient access in other than the primary clustered sequence can be efficiently achieved.

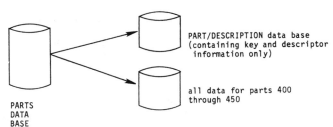

PARTS DATA BASE

PART/DESCRIPTION data base (containing key and descriptor information only)

all data for parts 400 through 450

Figure 2.23 Two ways of physically reducing the amount of data in the parts data base: stripping of descriptor into a separate data base and stripping all data for a range of key values into another data base.

PARTITIONING DATA BASES

The most significant factors to availability of data are data base size and the recovery and reorganization utilities required to support the data bases. While a data base is being recovered or reorganized, it is unavailable for otherwise normal processing. Therefore, two factors—data base size and complexity—greatly affect the elapsed time required for either utility. In general the more data and the more complex the structure (that is, the interrelationships of structures with other data bases), the longer the copy, recover, and reorganization utilities take to run.

One feature of DB2 is the ability to partition data bases. A data base that is going to contain a large amount of data may be divided into up to sixty-four separate partitions. The major advantage of a partition is that it can be reorganized or recovered independently of any other partition. If the damage or problem with a data base can be localized to a small amount of data, then only a few partitions of data need to be run under the recovery or reorganization utility. Figure 2.24 illustrates the partitioning of data under DB2.

Figure 2.24 shows the difference between a reorganization of a simple tablespace and a partitioned tablespace. The savings in terms of elapsed time required for reorganization is dramatic—from 10 hours to 10 minutes.

Of course, not all reorganizations can be restricted to a small (or single) number of partitions. In the case where all data must be reorganized (for example, when the structure of the data needs to be redefined), partitioning of data does not reduce the elapsed time needed to reorganize.

The factors that typically lead to a reorganization of data in DB2 include

- the need to reorganize data because of the internal disarray of data. For example, when more updates occur for a table than expected (especially more inserts of rows), then the pages of data and the indexes probably need to be reorganized.
- changing a nonclustered table to a clustered table. Rows need to be rearranged and the clustered index must be either built or reconstructed.
- changing of a field, indexed or otherwise. When the DDL definition of a field changes, the field must be converted to its new size, requiring a reloading into the new format.

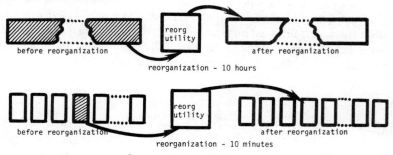

Figure 2.24 When data is partitioned and the cause for reorganization or recovery can be localized to a single partition (or a limited number of partitions), the amount of time needed to execute the utility is greatly reduced.

- changing of a field that is indexed. When the DDL definition of a field changes, the index on that field must be likewise changed and the data reloaded in the new format.
- addition of columns. If only a small number of rows will actually have data in the new columns, a reorganization of data may not be necessary, but if large amounts of data are involved in the addition of new columns of data, then a reorganization of the table is probably essential. However, it should be remembered that data cannot be redistributed and partitions cannot be added or deleted.

Even though data bases are connected by a foreign key in DB2 and in theory the connected data bases should never be out of synchronization, at the moment of reorganization it may be prudent and convenient to run a utility that cross-references data bases that are connected. Of course, this foreign key utility must be written by the application programmer.

Partitioning of data can be an asset for reasons other than data availability. Partitioning is for large data bases. The data can be broken up into two to sixty-four partitions. Each partition can be placed on a separate physical device. The separation across devices allows the data to be managed asynchronously and independently, thus reducing contention for access. In fact, access can take place in a parallel fashion, thus introducing the possibility of greatly reduced elapsed times in the processing of the access of a set of data. However, the column on which the data is partitioned, once partitioned, cannot be updated at the individual row level (that is, the row can be added or deleted, but not changed, because the column serves as the primary key and must maintain its uniqueness).

In addition, when data is partitioned, data that is highly accessed can be placed on high-performance DASD and data that has a lower probability of access can be placed on slower (or busier!) DASD. In such a manner, the performance of the system can be enhanced.

ENCODING OF DATA

The fewer number of tables, the fewer occasions to have to join relational data. One opportunity the designer has to minimize the number of tables without compromising the design of the system is to avoid encoded data.

A simple example of an encoded value would be the one byte of storage denoting either male or female—F or M. Another form of encoding might be

1. Headquarters, New York, New York
2. Branch Office, Detroit, Michigan
3. Field Office, El Paso, Texas

In general, when encoded values are used, there is no need to go from the encoded value to its transformation and in doing so use I/O.

However, the usage of encoded values is not quite as straightforward as the declaration that they should never be used. The designer should factor in the following considerations

- Some encoded values are commonly recognizable abbreviations, such as *F* for female and *M* for male. Self-evident encoded values can save space and require no I/O.
- Some encoded values are so commonly used within a company that a transformation from the encoded value to the actual value will seldom take place. In this case, encoding requires minimal I/O.
- Retrievals requiring translation (that is, lookup in separate tables) may be a small percentage of total retrievals required in processing the row. For example, a human resources system may encode job class to save space in each row, but only rarely will the printing of the actual job class be required.
- Encoding can save I/O in some cases. Suppose the headquarters of a company is at one location and is encoded as HDQTR throughout the system. When the headquarters is moved from Ithaca to Buffalo, the change in address need be made in only one place. All encoded references are still valid, even though the actual value has changed,
- The length of the encoded transformation may vary widely. This may (or may not) present special data management problems. When the data are encoded, the data management problems are minimized.

From the above discussion, it is clear that the decision to encode or not is a product of many factors. In general, encoding may cost I/O, but in special circumstances encoding offers other benefits that more than compensate for the I/O that might be consumed.

Summary

Data base design for DB2 assumes that the conceptual foundations for data are in place before the designer attempts to translate the requirements into a physical data base design. At the minimum, the conceptual foundation must include the separation of primitive and derived data, the subject orientation of primitive data, and the recognition and consolidation of commonality across disparate functional areas.

Once the conceptual requirements are in place, data elements are normalized and the denormalization process occurs. Denormalization is done in accordance with the frequency of usage of data.

An issue the physical designer faces is referential integrity, which in DB2 is entirely up to the application programmer. Referential integrity can be an impediment to performance and must be designed with the required underlying physical I/Os in mind.

Large data bases require special handling for reasons of performance and availability. In general, large collections of data should be broken up into multiple smaller collections of data.

Variable-length fields have their own performance implications. When a variable-length field is accessed and replaced with more data than were present when the variable field was accessed, then I/O is potentially needed for data management in the storage of the variable-length field.

Control data bases can become a bottleneck to performance when one or more applications are forced to single-thread through a control data base, especially when the control data base is being updated. Control data can be proliferated or broken into finer units of storage in order to expedite the flow through the data base.

Clustering of data, where applicable, can provide a means of minimizing I/O requirements when data are being sequentially accessed.

Encoding of data can harm performance if used improperly. Both CPU and I/O resources are used in the encoding and decoding of data.

CHAPTER 3
DB2 TRANSACTION DESIGN FOR PERFORMANCE

The first step in the achievement of consistent online performance in the DB2 production environment is the establishment of the appropriate environment. The next step is the proper design of applications. Application design has two components: data base design and transaction design. Data base design, discussed in Chapter 2, centers around arranging data so that a minimum of physical I/O is required in the access and update of data. Transaction design, an equal partner to data base design in the achievement of performance, is discussed in this chapter.

DB2 PERFORMANCE IN UNDESIGNED TRANSACTIONS

A *designed* transaction is one that is constructed in a disciplined manner to

- achieve the user's function
- use a minimal amount of resources

To build and maintain adequate DB2 online performance, all transactions running during the peak online period must be designed.

The importance of designed transactions being mixed in the online workload with undesigned transactions is best illustrated in terms of an example. Suppose a designed transaction, which uses a minimal amount of resources (that is I/Os), is represented by a small box or rectangle, analogically representing the usage of a small number of resources. Suppose an undesigned transaction, which uses an indeterminate number of resources—either large or small—is represented analogically by a large box or rectangle, which suggests the consumption of many resources. What happens when these two types of activities—designed and undesigned—are mixed in the same system? Figure 3.1 shows the results.

At 8 A.M. when the system is very lightly loaded and a few designed transactions are flowing through the system, system response time is 1 to 2 seconds. Note that machine utilization is around 10 percent to 15 percent in this time zone.

At 9 A.M. the system is fully loaded but is operating only on designed transactions. Response time is 4 to 5 seconds for all transactions, with machine utilization over 85 percent.

At 10 A.M. the system is at its peak usage. In the queue waiting to use the system are many designed transactions. In the processor are several undesigned transactions that are in execution. The system is running at the speed of the slowest activity in the system, which happens to be undesigned transactions. The speed of the undesigned transactions through the system is indeterminate.

Designed transactions that took 2 to 3 seconds at 8 A.M. may take 30 to 45 minutes at 10 A.M. The speed of the designed transactions through the system depends on queue time, which has nothing to do with the resources required by the transaction that is queued, but has everything to do with the resources required by the transactions queued in front of the transaction. (Note that the diagram at 10 A.M. is pedagogically designed to show the worst that can happen in online systems.) However, note that machine utilization is high throughout this period.

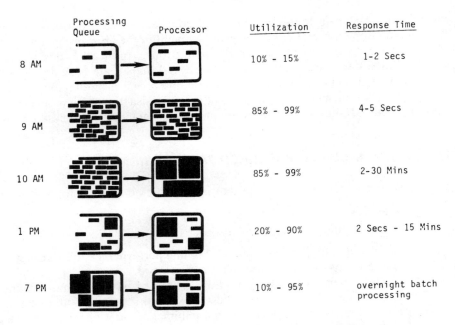

Figure 3.1 Processor utilization in the relational environment.

At 1 P.M. in a less fully loaded state, the system exhibits a fluctuating set of characteristics. Some of the time, when there are few undesigned transactions in the system, the system yields good response time; at other times, when there are many undesigned transactions in the system, the system yields spotty response time. Note that system utilization varies widely in this configuration.

DB2 performance in an unarchitected environment (that is, where designed and undesigned transactions are freely mixed) is said to fluctuate with the workload. In other words, when the workload has one makeup of transactions, response time is good; when the workload has another makeup of transactions, the response time is bad. The fairly normal state illustrated at 1 P.M. in Figure 3.1 reinforces this notion.

Finally, in the evening (in the case of the example, around 7 P.M.) the batch window begins, and the DB2 environment turns into an exclusively batch environment.

Why do fully loaded DB2 systems exhibit the performance characteristics described by the vignette in Figure 3.1, and what can be done about it?

WHY UNDESIGNED TRANSACTIONS IN DB2 DAMAGE ONLINE PERFORMANCE

In DB2, undesigned transactions damage overall system performance because of the queue time the undesigned transactions can cause for other transactions entering the system or executing after the undesigned transactions have gone into execution. In other words, a transaction's largest impediment to overall system performance is the resource utilization of the transactions that are queued in front.

As an illustration of this simple principle, suppose a person who wishes to cash a check goes into a bank and there are two lines—line A and line B—that the person may enter. Both lines are approximately the same length, and both lines are served by competent tellers who operate at roughly the same speed. Which line, then, should the person enter in order to get the best service and to cash his or her check the quickest?

Suppose in line A everyone wants to either cash a check or change a ten-dollar bill, activities that require only a small amount of time. Suppose in line B everyone except one person wishes to cash a check, but that one person wishes to balance his or her checkbook and verify every transaction for the last six months with the records of the bank. In this case, line B will be much slower than line A because of the nature of the activities of the people in the queue.

This simple bank queuing example illustrates the effect of placing an undesigned transaction in a queue with designed transactions. The designed transactions that are queued behind the undesigned transactions run at the speed of the undesigned transactions, which is slow.

WHAT TO DO ABOUT UNDESIGNED TRANSACTIONS

Several options in the management of undesigned transactions are

1. Recognize undesigned transactions as they enter the system, and do not allow them to be queued with designed transactions. This solution makes the assumption that undesigned transactions can be recognized prior to execution and that some queue for the slow transactions exists where the undesigned transactions can go without harm to performance.

   The first assumption—that undesigned transactions can be recognized upon entry into the system—is only partially true. Many transactions must go into execution before the resources used by the transaction are apparent, but by the time the transaction goes into execution it is too late to protect online resources.

   Furthermore, even if there were a way to recognize undesigned transactions, a considerable amount of resources are required because every transaction, upon entry to the system, must be analyzed to determine whether it is designed or undesigned.

   The second assumption is that there is a queue to which to send the undesigned transactions to get them out of the way of the designed transactions. If the undesigned queue is one that runs after hours, then there is no problem with online performance. Unfortunately, the problem arises that a user who submits an undesigned transaction must wait until the next day to receive the output from his or her request for processing.

   Assigning all undesigned transactions to their own queue, and then letting the queue operate on online data bases in tandem with queues that hold designed transactions opens up other impediments to performance.

Shared buffer pools, disk access of data (that is, arm and head movement), and internal integrity mechanisms and facilities are all shared by online queues of transactions, whether the queue is designed or not. Consequently, performance exposures abound even when undesigned transactions are removed to their own queue and are allowed to access commonly shared data on the same processor as designed transactions.

2. Allow the system to page undesigned transactions out whenever the system reaches the state portrayed by 10 A.M. in Figure 3.1. Certainly when the undesigned transaction is paged out, designed transactions are allowed to flow through the system quickly. However, there are some major drawbacks to paging as a solution to performance. The first and most obvious is the resources required for paging.

   Paging causes physical I/O just like a regular read or write of a data base, but the problems of paging run deeper. Not all undesigned transactions can be conveniently paged out.

   Suppose an undesigned transaction is updating an entire data base and is partially through with the update. To maintain integrity of the data, either all of the data base updates must be backed out or all data that has been updated and potentially can be updated must be protected against further access or update until the paged program can be re-entered into the system. In the case in which paging occurs and data are left protected, if one of the transactions to be executed needs to go against the data that has been protected, then deadlock occurs and a real performance bottleneck is created. In the case in which a massive backout of data base updates occurs, the resource requirements are tremendous. An irony is that once the program is paged back in, the updates must be reapplied once again, using even more resources.

   Because of the automatic inefficiencies of paging and the problems of data base update integrity, paging is not a popular option.

3. Separation of designed and undesigned transactions by the end user at the moment of entry into the online system. Another option, which realistically has limited applicability, is to require the end user to separate designed transactions from undesigned transactions prior to entry into the online system. Surprisingly, when this option is applicable, it is a very plausible solution. Unfortunately this option is applicable only infrequently. Requiring end users to separate designed transactions from undesigned transactions requires an end user who is both sophisticated and motivated.

   Most users lack the background to be able to distinguish an undesigned transaction from a designed transaction. Even when the end user can make this distinction, the end user is hard-pressed to say why the separation should be made.

   Furthermore, suppressing the submissions of transactions requires a user to sacrifice immediate personal needs for the good of the online community. Most end users do not understand or support such approaches.

Consequently, voluntary separation of end user requests based on resource consumption is an infrequently chosen option.

4. Creating designed transactions from undesigned transactions at the design level and allowing only designed transactions to run online in the peak processing period is another option. This option in the long run easily is the most effective (and ironically the least expensive) option.

   Furthermore, every undesigned transaction can be broken into a series of designed transactions, although at first this transformation capability is not apparent. More importantly, the notion of transforming undesigned transactions into designed transactions fits very closely with the establishment of the production environment, as has been discussed.

CHARACTERISTICS OF DESIGNED AND UNDESIGNED TRANSACTIONS

The preceding discussion explains why online systems are so sensitive to designed and undesigned transactions. In short, under any volume of processing, DB2 cannot tolerate undesigned transactions and sustain good online performance.

What are the characteristics of designed and undesigned transactions in DB2? The primary difference between designed and undesigned transactions is the resource consumption of the transaction, and resource consumption revolves primarily around the I/Os consumed.

In general a designed transaction will consume no more than ten physical I/Os per execution of the transaction. An undesigned transaction may consume an indeterminate number of I/Os—from 15 to more than 15,000.

DATA-DRIVEN PROCESSES

A word of caution is in order concerning a special class of transactions. Some undesigned transactions consume a small amount of I/O in some cases, and in other cases, depending upon the data on which they are operating, consume large amounts of I/O. Such transactions are referred to as *data-driven processes*.

For example, suppose a canned query is made by which a bank teller can query the monthly activity for an account. John Jones queries his account in four I/Os. Mary Smith queries her account in six I/Os. The accounts receivable clerk for IBM queries the IBM account in 15,000 I/Os. The amount of resource consumption of any given transaction depends not as much on the efficiency of the calls of the transaction or the optimization of the efficiency of the path of calls but on the amount of data on which the transactions operate.

The amount of resource consumption of a data-driven transaction depends on the data on which the transaction operates, not on any superficial analysis by a call optimizer. Data-driven transactions are one of the variables that make distinguishing designed transactions from undesigned transactions prior to execution very difficult.

I/Os

I/Os, then, are the primary resource consumed by transactions that separate designed transactions from undesigned transactions. Why is I/O the most critical factor?

I/Os are critical because they operate at mechanical speeds—in the millisecond range. Other computer operations operate in the electrical range—at nanosecond speeds. Electronic speeds are about two to three orders of magnitude faster than mechanical speeds. Consequently, the flow of activities in an online environment is constrained by I/O because of the mechanical nature of I/O.

However, I/O consumption, as singularly important as it is, is not the only reason why undesigned transactions throttle performance.

DATA CONTENTION

Consider the probability of contention for data in the light of undesigned and designed transactions. A designed transaction accesses a limited amount of data and the chances are good that it will not try to access data that are already locked by another online transaction. Furthermore, the designed transaction will lock up only a small amount of data. Finally, because the designed transaction executes only a few instructions, the designed transaction locks up its data for only a short amount of time.

Now consider undesigned transactions. An undesigned transaction accesses much data. Consequently, the odds are good that the undesigned transaction will attempt to access data that already are locked by another transaction. The differences between designed and undesigned transactions are illustrated by Figures 3.2 and 3.3.

Because the undesigned transaction runs for a long period of time, the odds are good that the locked data will be locked for a long period of time. All of these factors increase the probability of contention for data in the online environment.

The solution to contention is obvious: Simply do not allow undesigned transactions to run during the peak period of processing when online response time is critical.

Transaction Issues

The DB2 language—SQL—operates on sets of data, not on records of data. To achieve good performance, the designer must structure the usage of SQL so that only very limited sets of data can be retrieved or operated on.

Some of the techniques for minimizing the resources used by a transaction are

- Do not use language structures such as AVERAGE and SUM, that will require full or partial data base scans.

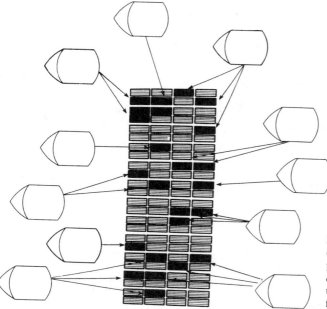

Figure 3.2   When each online user requests a limited amount of data, the probability of conflicting with the needs of another user is greatly minimized, thus reducing the number of lock conflicts.

- Do not use search criteria based on nonindexed fields.
- Fully qualify every SQL query so that the absolute minimum of data is accessed. Ideally one row will satisfy every SQL call.
- When multiple SQL rows are needed, access data as if it were clustered.

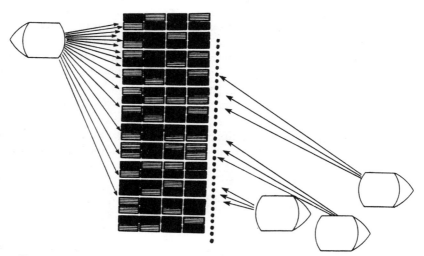

Figure 3.3   When one program accesses and locks much data, other programs experience poor performance as they wait for the long-running program to complete execution.

- When multiple SQL rows are needed, retrieve no more than ten rows per execution of the transaction.
- When data must be accessed sequentially on a nonclustered field, access no more than ten rows for each iteration of the transaction.
- When views are used, do not use views that access data across multiple tables.
- When foreign keys must be used to relate data, do not use the foreign key relationships more than ten times in the execution of the transaction.
- Do not access data through QMF; use embedded SQL in COBOL or PL-1 only.
- Do not do relational joins or projects during the online peak-period processing.
- Do not do DDL processing during peak-period processing.

EXAMPLES OF DESIGNED AND UNDESIGNED TRANSACTIONS

The following illustrates what a designed transaction looks like and how an undesigned transaction may be transformed into a designed transaction. Consider the access of the simple data base shown in Figure 3.4.

An example of a designed transaction might be

```
SELECT PARTNO QOH DESC
FROM PARTABLE
WHERE PART = '515-q'
```

The result of the transaction is "515-q, 50000, joint."

From a resource utilization perspective, the question becomes, What amount of I/O was required to process the simple transaction?

Every transaction has a certain amount of overhead I/O; receiving the query from the terminal and sending results back to the terminal represent I/O that is required for every transaction regardless of any other activities. This ordinary I/O—as long as it is not excessive—is not of great concern to the system developer. Instead, the system developer addresses the incremental I/O used by a transaction.

In the case of the example, one I/O is required to access the index looking for the key—part number 515-q—assuming the index has not been placed entirely

Part	Description	U/M	Class	QOH
461-J	Mold	unit	p	45
491-A	Bed	unit	p	13
513-I	Casing	unit	p	186
515-Q	Joint	vat	np	50000
521-T	Brace	box	np	106
521-X	Y-brace	box	np	35
⋮	⋮	⋮	⋮	⋮

Figure 3.4 Part number/Inventory table—primary key—part number, clustered.

in memory, which is not likely for an index for a large production data base. The I/O to the index yields the page number needed, and another I/O is done to find the page that contains the row being sought.

If by chance the page being sought were already in the buffer area, no I/O would be needed. In all, a maximum of two data base I/Os will be required to service the transaction, which is easily within the bounds of a designed transaction.

As long as all online transactions are within the boundaries of a designed transaction (as far as resource consumption is concerned), DB2 performance will be optimal.

Contrast the simple designed transaction described above with the following data-driven, undesigned transaction. Using the data base shown in Figure 3.4 and assuming that there is an index on description, the following SQL request is made

```
SELECT PARTNO QOH
FROM PARTABLE
WHERE DESC = 'NUT'
```

The amount of I/O needed to satisfy this request is indeterminate and potentially large. If there are 500 parts that satisfy the criteria and if 3 index pages must be read, then 503 I/Os will need to be done (discounting a few fortuitous hits in the buffer). If there are 10 parts with a description of NUT, then 10 I/Os plus at least one I/O for the index will be required.

In short, not until the transaction goes into execution will it be known whether the transaction is going to violate the criteria for being designed or undesigned, but certainly more than 500 I/Os violate the criteria for being a designed transaction. (This transaction is a classical example of a data-driven transaction and illustrates the difficulty of predetermining designed and undesigned transactions prior to execution).

A third type of transaction is illustrated by the request

```
SELECT COUNT (*)
FROM PARTABLE
WHERE CLASS = 'P'
```

In this case the analyst wishes to determine how many parts have been classified as precious goods (where class = P). Assume that no index exists on class because it is a commonly occurring value.

The number of I/Os required is the number of pages in the data base. If the data base is large and there are 1500 pages, then 1500 I/Os will be required. Unlike the previously discussed transaction which, depending on the data, may or may not require much I/O, this transaction will be an undesigned transaction for anything but the smallest of tables.

To achieve good, consistent online performance, none of the undesigned transactions can be allowed to execute during online, peak-period processing.

CREATING DESIGNED TRANSACTIONS

The first question the developer must ask is whether large batch sequential scans of data should be done during peak-period processing in the first place. Philosophically, what is the business function served by batch sequential scans and are those scans cost-justified? This topic must be thoroughly addressed before proceeding. In general, most sequential processing will be relegated to the off-hours processing window.

If the user absolutely insists on doing large, batch-oriented data base scans online, then at the very least those scans must be repackaged to fit within the requirements of the peak-period processing window.

Controlling resource consumption under DB2 is difficult but not impossible, because SQL does processing of data set at a time. To illustrate the difficulty of the control of resource utilization under normal SQL, consider the following simple SQL program operating against the table found in Figure 3.4.

```
SELECT PARTNO
FROM PARTABLE
WHERE CLASS = 'P' AND PARTNO < '1000'
```

Such an SQL statement would effectively retrieve only parts with a key less than 1,000, where class equals *P* and probably, depending on the database, use a modest amount of I/O, however DB2 chose to access the data. The number of parts retrieved depends upon knowledge of the data base. If there are few parts from a key range of 0000 to 1000, then the query will use few resources. If there are many parts between 0000 and 1000, then the selection criteria can be narrowed down to a smaller range, say from 000 to 100. Of course, intelligent range selection of this type depends on the data being indexed and clustered by part number.

However, the program would be a strange one indeed because undoubtedly many other parts exist that satisfy the criterion beyond the key range selected.

In the spirit of using a small amount of resources for each online execution, if the user wished to continue to scan the data, then the user can remember the location of the last part number accessed, go to that part, and sequentially scan some more parts.

Suppose part 1258-QX were the last part retrieved. The following SQL program could then be used to continue the batch scan

```
SELECT PARTNO
FROM PARTABLE
WHERE CLASS = 'P' AND
PARTNO BETWEEN '01258-QX' AND '02000-ZZ'
```

This process (where the parameters of the set being accessed are reset for every execution) could be iterated for as long as the end user desired, retrieving a small amount of data in each execution of the program and beginning each execution where the previous one left off.

As long as data were being accessed along its clustered field, then the number of parts to be retrieved per iteration may be substantial. Fifty or sixty parts could be retrieved for each iteration because less I/O will be required in going from one clustered part to the next.

However, the simple approach described here has some pitfalls. Between executions the data that are being queried may be updated. For example, suppose in iteration n the last part number retrieved was 9409-MZ. Immediately after the nth execution, the part number was deleted by some other transaction. On the n + 1 iteration, when the user tries to position the program to part 9409-MZ, there will be no part for repositioning.

Another assumption the technique of reiterating a large scan of data makes is that the same PLAN will be used for each execution. Under normal conditions this assumption will be true, but there is no reason why the PLAN may not be changed from one iteration to the next.

The technique described here—that of iterating through a batch sequential scan—has the advantage of requiring a limited amount of resources and freezing those resources for only a short while. Unfortunately, effective execution of this technique requires a detailed knowledge of the data that are being operated on.

As such, the technique of reiterating a large scan of data can transform an undesigned transaction into a designed transaction, but a certain amount of overhead is associated with the technique. DB2, like all online software, requires a certain amount of initiation and shutdown processing. Each iteration requires this overhead.

Care must be taken with the coding techniques used in the iterating by the end user through a data base scan, because DB2 may not yield the desired performance in every case. Consider what would happen if the data were not indexed and clustered. Suppose a very simple SQL query were issued.

```
SELECT PARTNO UM
FROM PARTABLE
WHERE CLASS = 'P' AND
         UM BETWEEN 'TON' AND 'YARD'
```

In this case DB2 will scan the entire data base for *every* execution of the query, regardless of where the parameters of set delineation are set.

Another approach is to execute only so many instructions and then automatically require the end user to continue processing in off-hours. For example, the (pseudo) SQL program accomplishes this objective:

```
SELECT PARTNO
FROM PARTABLE
WHERE PARTNO < '1000'
    (issue message to continue
       processing offline if more
       parts are desired)
```

Because sets of data are scanned by DB2 and DB2 has limited facilities for monitoring resources used, controlling resource utilization of nonindexed, non-clustered data is very difficult. However, if the designer knows that there is a large amount of unclustered data with like values to be accessed, at the application level the designer can artificially introduce criteria that will force sets of data to be subdivided. As a simple example, consider a personnel data base that has employees classified either as male or female (that is, the field for SEX contains the values M or F).

Any query against the personnel file using sex as a criteria will result in a large number of rows satisfying the criteria and the entire data base being scanned. However, suppose an artificial classification were introduced for an employee (call the artificial field ECLASS for employee class). For the first fifty employees the value of 1 is assigned as their classification. For the next fifty employees a value of 2 is assigned, and so forth. Now assume an index is created on SEX and ECLASS. A query can now be done so that SQL does not yield a huge result and a subset of the data base can be scanned in an iterative fashion:

```
SELECT EMPNAME SEX DOHIRE
FROM EMPTABLE
WHERE SEX = 'M' AND ECLASS = 1
```

This query will yield all the men with ECLASS = 1, roughly twenty-five rows on the average, assuming about as many women employees as men employees. To retrieve the next set of men employees, ECLASS = 2 is used as the qualifier, and so forth. In such a fashion an indexed, unclustered table can be iteratively accessed without using a damaging amount of I/O. Note that without an index on SEX and ECLASS that the entire data base must be scanned with each iteration, certainly defeating the purpose of managing online resources.

The update of ECLASS is an issue using the above scheme. Because ECLASS is artificial, the accuracy of the data is not terribly important; individual inserts and deletes, as long as there are not too many of them, do not affect the usefulness of the field. On occasion it will be useful to create a batch program (running during the off-peak hours) that will sequentially scan the data base and reset ECLASS.

In fact, when the selection is based entirely on unindexed fields, the entire data base must be scanned. Breaking large scans into a series of smaller scans is practically impossible.

A variation of this same technique is possible if an arbitrary division of data already exists and is indexed and clustered. For example, suppose EMPLNO is an indexed, clustered field and is unique to every employee. The following query effectively separates employees into manageable subsets of data.

```
SELECT EMPNAME SEX DOHIRE
FROM EMPTABLE
WHERE SEX = 'M' AND
          EMPNO BETWEEN 000 AND 100
```

This query could be expected to receive about fifty replies and operate on only a subset of the data base. As employee number goes from 1 to 100 and so on, a manageable number of I/Os is consumed for each iteration.

Another approach to controlling the I/O done by a SQL program is to break down function very finely. Suppose the functional specifications were issued for a SQL program, as shown in Figure 3.5.

Functional Specifications for a SQL Program

o Locate Part number
o Update Part number quantity
o Locate Supplier for Part Number
o Get Supplier discount, price, eoq, shipping data
o Issue Purchase order
o Send Invoice data to Accounts Payable
o Update inventory
o Prepare Shipping dock reception

The functional specifications can be broken up
into several SQL programs -

SQL program 1 -
```
o Locate Part number
o Update Part number quantity
```

SQL program 2 -
```
o Locate Supplier for Part number
o Get Supplier discount, price, eoq, shipping data
o Issue Purchase order
```

SQL program 3 -
```
o Send Invoice to Accounts Payable
```

SQL program 4 -
```
o Update Inventory
o Prepare Shipping Dock reception
```

Figure 3.5 Breaking a large amount of function that is accomplished in a single program into a series of transactions that collectively accomplish the same thing.

Figure 3.5 shows that the function accomplished by SQL processing has been broken into a series of smaller processes that accomplish the same thing. There are many advantages to the separation of function into small components. The first and most obvious advantage is that performance is greatly enhanced in that all processing during peak period is designed. The resources required by any given program in execution are much less than the resources required by the large conglomeration of requirements taken together. The amount of data held by a PLAN is much less than if all the requirements were conglomerated.

There are other advantages as well. In the case of the example in Figure 3.5, when a problem is encountered in the middle of the execution of processing, the entire processing that has already occurred must be backed out. When functions are broken down into fine units of execution, the problems that occur can be resolved without backing out otherwise validly processed data.

Care must be taken in using iterations of transactions to scan a large data base because in some cases iterating transactions can cost I/O and actually hurt performance. Suppose the simple data base, as depicted in Figure 3.6 is to be scanned.

The data base depicted in Figure 3.6 is a very large data base. A query is to be run against the data base seeking all activities of the amount $74.32. The first query against the data base looks like:

```
SELECT ACCT ACTDATE LOCATION
FROM ACTABLE
WHERE AMT = 74.32 AND
        ACCT BETWEEN 000 AND 100
```

ACCT	ACTDATE	AMT	LOCATION	ID
0129	860103	12308.90	Fremont	IP
0129	860103	300.00	Fremont	TR
0129	860104	74.32	San Jose	UY
0129	860110	25.00	Sunnyvale	--
⋮	⋮	⋮	⋮	⋮

ACCT	ACTDATE	AMT	LOCATION	ID
0129	861006	2009.08	Fremont	LK
0129	861008	25.00	Sunnyvale	PL
0129	861019	150.00	Fremont	--
0129	861021	209.00	Santa Cruz	LL
⋮	⋮	⋮	⋮	⋮

Figure 3.6 Indexed, clustered on ACCT, ACTDATE.

This first query against the data base will access the pages and index for all accounts between 000 and 100—in all, the activity of at most 100 accounts. Depending upon the density and population of the activities and the accounts (that is, how many activities per account there are and how many accounts there are), a modest amount of I/O will be used.

Now, consider the I/O required for the nth iteration of the scan (for the purpose of this example, $m = n + 1$).

```
SELECT ACCT ACTDATE LOCATION
FROM ACTABLE
WHERE AMT = 74.32 AND
      ACCT BETWEEN n00 AND m00
```

The number of pages to be accessed is the same as in the first iteration, but the index must be rescanned for each iteration. Each iteration causes DB2 to rescan the index from the beginning of the index. Even with a hierarchical index, the amount of I/O used to scan the index mounts up in the face of a very large data base. For small data bases and small indexes, this repositioning of the transaction for each iteration of processing presents no problem, but for large amounts of data, such is not the case.

The repositioning of each transaction in the data base for iterative processing of the data base points out one of the difficulties of managing large data bases in DB2. Of course, the data base could be broken into a series of smaller data bases, and many of the performance problems would be minimized.

In the example shown, only the index had to be rescanned for each iteration of the transaction. Suppose the designer had used a selection criterion such that the index was not used by DB2. In this case, the entire data base (that is, the pages) must be rescanned from the start for every iteration of the query.

Static or Dynamic SQL

Another SQL option the designer has is to execute STATIC or DYNAMIC SQL statements. Under normal conditions STATIC SQL will be executed online, in the fashion associated with standard online transaction processing. Under STATIC

SQL the embedded SQL is prepared for execution so that at the moment of execution very little transaction preparation is required.

Under DYNAMIC SQL the syntax of SQL can be either changed or created prior to the execution of the transaction. Upon completion of the modification or entry of the SQL text, a substantial amount of overhead is incurred in preparation for execution. DYNAMIC SQL is typical of the processing found in the interactive environment, not the online environment. The overhead of preparation for execution for DYNAMIC SQL is such that only under the most extreme or unusual cases should DYNAMIC SQL be used in the online environment.

EMBEDDED SQL

All production DB2 processing is done from embedded SQL. To that end, the developer needs to be familiar with the mechanics of embedded SQL. The following is a brief description of the language mechanics required to use DB2 in the production online environment.

Embedded SQL operates (usually) out of a PL-1 or COBOL program. The following shows a simple example of the mechanics of how embedded SQL in a PL-1 program retrieves a single row of data.

```
(PLISQLPG; PROC OPTIONS (MAIN);
DCL PARTNO CHAR(10);
EXEC SQL INCLUDE PARTABLE;
END-EXEC.
EXEC SQL INCLUDE SQLCA;
END-EXEC.
        .       .       .       .       .       .
        .       .       .       .       .       .
        .       .       .       .       .       .
        GET LIST (PARTNO);
        EXEC SQL SELECT PARTROW INTO = :PARTROW
                    FROM PARTABLE
                    WHERE PART = :PARTNO;
        IF SQLCODE = 0
                THEN PUT EDIT (PARTROW)
                                        (A(25));
        ELSE
            PUT EDIT ('SQL ERROR CODE IS:', SQLCODE)
                        (A(18), F(10));
        END-EXEC.
        .       .       .       .       .       .
        .       .       .       .       .       .
        .       .       .       .       .       .
```

In the program example shown, a single row would be processed by the PL-1 program. What if more than one row might be returned by the SQL program?

The following skeleton program illustrates the technique for executing a program that accesses multiple rows.

```
(PLISQLPG:    PROC OPTIONS (MAIN);
DCL PARTNO CHAR(10);
EXEC SQL INCLUDE PARTABLE;
END-EXEC.
EXEC SQL INCLUDE SQLCA;
END-EXEC.
EXEC SQL DECLARE A CURSOR FOR
                SELECT COUNT(*)
                FROM PARTABLE
                WHERE PART = :PARTNO;
END-EXEC.
        .     .     .     .     .     .     .
        .     .     .     .     .     .     .
EXEC SQL OPEN A;
END-EXEC.
        .     .     .     .     .     .     .
        .     .     .     .     .     .     .
        DO WHILE (SQLCODE = 0);
EXEC SQL
        FETCH A INTO :PARTABLE;
END-EXEC.
            .     .     .     .      .;
            .     .     .     .      .;
    . . . . . . . . . . . . . . . . . .
    . . . . . . . . . . . . . . . . . .
    . . . . . . . . . . . . . . . . . .
EXEC SQL CLOSE A;
END-EXEC.
END;
```

The SQLCA area is a commonly included reference to the SQL communications area. The values returned in the communications area determine the validity or success of the SQL call just completed. A SQLCODE value of 0 indicates a normal completion with a new row returned.

For a complete, more detailed description of all the programming techniques and the meaning of the different statements, refer to the application programming guides (IMS, CICS, and so on) mentioned in the references.

Summary

The second major issue of design for performance is that of transaction design, which calls for the creation of designed transactions. A *designed transaction* is one that uses a limited amount of resources. Only designed transactions will be allowed to run in the online production environment. The essence of designed transactions is to break large amounts of function into smaller subsets or to execute long-running transactions in a series of small iterations.

One of the difficulties of DB2 transaction performance is that SQL operates only on sets of records at a time. To achieve good performance, the sets of records must be broken into subsets.

It is assumed that certain resource-intensive commands, such as SORT, SUM, and AVG, will not be executed in online processing.

CHAPTER 4
DETAILED DESIGN AND TUNING

The performance of DB2 is sensitive to the detailed operations of the computer as it executes the instructions issued by DB2. The data base designer must be aware of the underlying activities that occur as a result of processing DB2. Some of the finer points the designer should be aware of are included in this chapter.

USING AN INDEX

DB2 elects when to use or not use an index. The choice is not controlled by the programmer. Whether an index is used or not makes a big difference to system performance in terms of I/O consumption. The following discussion outlines some of the instances when DB2 may not use an index. The prudent designer shows careful consideration

PART	DESCR	QTY	U/M
01258	Ball bearing	1900	box
21340-A	Housing mold	17	unit
00897-B	Rear End Assem	891	unit
98005-A	Idler Arm	67	unit

```
SELECT PARTNO
FROM PARTABLE
WHERE PARTNO = DESCR
```

Figure 4.1

- of comparing different columns within the same row, as illustrated by Figure 4.1. In this example, even if the columns PARTNO and DESCR are indexed, a row-by-row search will be done.
- of comparing different character columns where the columns have different lengths. In the example shown in Figure 4.2, two tables are being compared, but the field over which they are being compared is character and has a different length. Consequently, an index comparison will not be made even if the index exists.
- for indexes over multiple columns. The highest order column must be qualified by " = " as shown in Figure 4.3, a table that will be searched row by row.

PARTINV TABLE

PARTNO	QTY		PARTBOM PARTRAW	EXPEDITE	DESCR
01258-QX	90		99020	J Jones	Ball bearing
08797-A	179		99801-Y	S Smith	Camshaft
990-AQ14	16		00198-S	J Wilson	Differential
00178-UT	3		9980-G	J Jones	Throwbolt

8 bytes   7 bytes

```
SELECT PARTNO QTY EXPEDITE DESCR
FROM PARTINV, PARTBOM
WHERE PARTNO = PARTRAW
```

Figure 4.2

YR*	Mon*	DAY*	ACCOUNT	LOCATION	AMOUNT	TYPE	ID	TELLER
86	12	28	001567	San Mateo	189.87	Nor	JG	------
86	12	26	001567	Burlngame	90.25	Nor	KY	0067
86	11	17	001789	Oakland	1000.00	--	LP	0081
86	11	13	000019	Palo Alto	75.00	Nor	PE	------
86	09	27	100989	Fremont	750.00	--	GF	0081

*- index on these columns in the order shown

```
SELECT YR MON DAY ACCOUNT ID AMOUNT
FROM BANK.ACTIVITY
WHERE MONTH > 01 AND DAY = 20
```

Figure 4.3

- of the precision and scale of a decimal field affects whether or not an index will be used. Figure 4.4 illustrates the possibilities. When odd precision is specified, as in MOQ, an index may be used. When even precision is specified, an index will not be used except where precision is zero and ORDER BY is specified, in which case the index may be used.

- if a literal or variable is being compared to a column and the literal or variable is greater than the column in length, then an index will not be used, as specified in Figure 4.5. Here the variable being compared to a column is greater than 10 bytes and the column length is 10 bytes. As a result, an index will not be used in the comparison.

- if numeric fields are being compared and the precision of the literal or host variable is greater than that of the column key being compared, then an index will not be used. Figure 4.6 shows a literal of 10.5 being compared to

PARTNO	DESCR	QOM	EOQ	MOQ
001258-QX	Ball bearing	789	125.98	130.00
887001-I	Housing mold	19	23.75	26.79
001670-YR	Drive train	1009	1897.08	1908.96
00002	Camshaft	9	6.90	6.78

| char 15 | char 15 | decimal (6,0) | decimal (6,2) | decimal (7,2) |

```
SELECT PARTNO DESCR QOM
FROM PARTINV                    (will not use index)
WHERE EOQ<= 15

SELECT PARTNO DESCR QOM
FROM PARTINV                    (may use index)
ORDER BY QOM

SELECT PARTNO DESCR QOM
FROM PARTINV                    (will not use index)
WHERE QOM  = 15

SELECT PARTNO DESCR QOM
FROM PARTINV                    (may use index)
WHERE MOQ <= 25
```

Figure 4.4

PARTNO	DESCR	UM	QOH
001258-QX	Bearing	un	1000
800879-UR	Housing	un	980
801258-P	Idle arm	box	87
900001	Tappet	bin	66
:	:	:	:
:	:	:	:

```
SELECT PARTNO DESCR QOH
FROM PARTINV
WHERE DESCR = 'Housing mold box'
```

char 10

Figure 4.5

a column of decimal 7,0. An index will not be used in this case.

- if comparison is done on an expression, an index (or indexes) will not be used, as shown in Figure 4.7.
- if the potential for update exists, the query will not use an index. Figure 4.8 shows the packaging of functions together (including some updating functions) such that all functions packaged together will be unable to use an index. When the functions shown in Figure 4.8 are broken into smaller packages, the effect of not being able to use an index is spread over a smaller amount of data.

PARTNO	DESCR	UM	QOH
001258-QX	Ball bearing	un	670
800907	Camshaft	un	97
000789-TR	Pulley	un	90
900001	Tappet	box	100
:	:	:	:
:	:	:	:

```
SELECT PARTNO DESCR QOH
FROM PARTINV
WHERE QOH < = 10.5
```

decimal
(7,0)

Figure 4.6

The reader is alerted to the fact that not all instances of index usage have been covered in this section. Furthermore, unlike basic concepts that are not release dependent, the treatment of indexes by DB2 is highly release dependent. The

PARTNO	QOH	DESCR	UM	QINSTORE	QDEL	QISSUED
001258-QX	13	ball bearing	un	500	67	130
800906	120	carburetor	un	70	0	0
800070-TW	7	rocker arm	box	3	1	0
900001	0	manifold	kit	28	3	0
009075-PY	16	piston ring	kit	108	0	15
:	:	:	:	:	:	:
:	:	:	:	:	:	:

```
SELECT PARTNO DESCR
FROM PARTINV                                    (index not used)
WHERE QOH = QINSTORE + QDEL - QISSUED
```

Figure 4.7

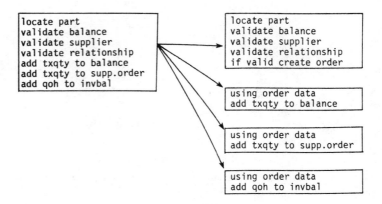

Figure 4.8 Packaging function into smaller packages causes the system to function more efficiently, including allowing indexes to be used where they otherwise would not have been used.

reader is referred to the section on index utilization in the IBM manual "Application Design and Tuning Guide, GG24-3004."

INDEXING VARIABLE LENGTH COLUMNS

When an index is created for variable-length columns, the index is "filled out," (that is, padded) so that all index entries are of the maximum length, as shown in Figure 4.9. This figure shows the index entries as they exist in the index and as they exist in the data base.

Because of the padding effect, if the maximum length is long, an index on variable length columns is questionable. A viable option is to break the variable-length column into two or more columns and to index only one of the columns, which has the effect of creating a smaller index.

DEFINING VARIABLE LENGTH FIELDS

All variable length fields should be defined at the end of the row after fixed length fields, as shown in Figure 4.10. When variable length fields are defined at the end of a row, fewer system resources are required in accessing fixed length fields than if the variable length fields were defined at the first of the row.

```
PARTNO      QOH     DESCR                                    INDEX
                                                 :     :     :     :
001258-QX|  15      |ball bearing|
800974-P  1100      |manifold housing and brace|    ball¢bearing¢¢¢¢¢¢¢¢¢¢¢¢
007097-LK|   0      |differential assembly|         dealer¢housing¢¢¢¢¢¢¢¢¢¢¢
001349-IT|  19      |dealer housing|
                                                 differential¢assembly¢¢¢¢¢
     :       :          :                                               ¢ = blank
     :       :          :
     :       :          :        manifold¢housing¢and¢brace
     :       :          :               :     :     :     :     :
```
Figure 4.9

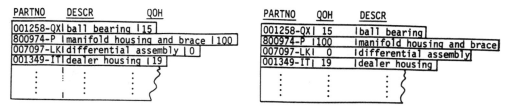

Figure 4.10

DECIMAL DATA DEFINITION

Decimal data should be defined in odd precision only, because storage requirements will be the same even if the precision is defined with even precision, and because of index utilization of odd precision decimal data. Figure 4.11 illustrates the storage required for odd and even decimal utilization.

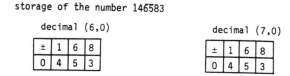

storage of the number 146583

decimal (6,0)

±	1	6	8
0	4	5	3

decimal (7,0)

±	1	6	8
0	4	5	3

Figure 4.11 Data stored on the left has a specification of decimal (6,0) and data stored on the right has a specification of decimal (7,0), but both specifications require the same amount of space.

INDEX SPACE CONSIDERATIONS

The amount of space required for an index must be factored into the total system requirements in several ways. For example, consider the two tables shown in Figure 4.12.

One index—on accounts—requires only a nominal amount of space. The other index—on names—requires much space because of the length of the field.

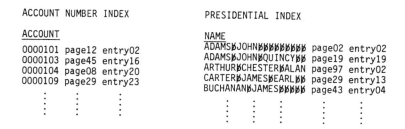

ACCOUNT NUMBER INDEX

ACCOUNT
0000101 page12 entry02
0000103 page45 entry16
0000104 page08 entry20
0000109 page29 entry23

PRESIDENTIAL INDEX

NAME
ADAMSβJOHNββββββββββ page02 entry02
ADAMSβJOHNβQUINCYββ page19 entry19
ARTHURβCHESTERβALAN page97 entry02
CARTERβJAMESβEARLββ page29 entry13
BUCHANANβJAMESββββ page43 entry04

Figure 4.12 When an index is built, the amount of data required for the field on which the index is built must be factored into the space requirements. If the field is large, then much space will be required just for the index alone.

```
                              Data Before Update
INDEX                    PARTNO   QOH  UM  DESCRIPTION
  :    :    :    :         :       :   :       :    :
part1250 page45 entry13   1247    4501 kit ball joint
  :    :    :    :         1250    100  bin pipe fitting      page45
                          1253      69  box tail assembly     entry13
                           :       :    :    :    :    :
```

```
                              Data After Update
INDEX                    PARTNO   QOH  UM  DESCRIPTION
  :    :    :    :         :       :   :       :    :
part1250 page45 entry13   1247    4501 kit ball joint         page45
  :    :    :    :        page59 entry26                      entry13
                          1253      69  box tail assembly
                           :       :    :    :    :    :


                         PARTNO   QOH  UM  DESCRIPTION
                           :       :   :       :    :
                          1250    100  bin pipe fitting tee joint  page59
                           :       :    :    :    :    :            entry26
```

Figure 4.13

UPDATING VARIABLE-LENGTH FIELDS

When variable-length fields are updated and the variable field takes up more space than it did prior to update, then the row may be placed in another page if not enough space exists to fully replace the row in the original page, as shown in Figure 4.13.

In Figure 4.13, the index for part 1250 is page 45, entry 13. Then the inventory control clerk decides to add more information to the description field, changing the description to "pipe fitting tee joint." Unfortunately, there is not enough space in row 45 to allow the row to be replaced, so available space is sought elsewhere and is located in page 59. The row is placed in page 59 and a pointer from page 45 to page 59 is created. However, the index entry points to page 45. Now two I/Os (three, counting index access) are required to access part 1250.

INDEXING SMALL DATA BASES

In the case where there are not many pages of data in a data base (which is seldom the case in the production environment), the usage and existence of an index is questionable. It may be more efficient just to access the small data base each time it is desired to access any data in the data base than it is to create, maintain, and use indexes on the small data base. Figure 4.14 illustrates the trade-offs associated with a small data base and indexing.

Figure 4.14 shows a small data base with six pages and four rows per page. An index is shown pointing into the data base. The index is on "unit of measure," which is not a field the data base is clustered on.

Two series of activities against the data base are shown: one series of activities using an index and another series of activities not using an index. In the activities using the index, I/Os are done to bring the index into the buffer area, and

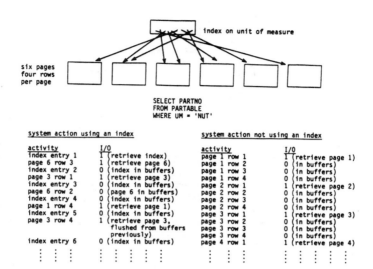

Figure 4.14   The activities of the processor as an indexed and a nonindexed data base are being read. The activities are requested by the data base management system in response to the programs being executed. Adjacent to the activity are the physical I/O events stimulated by the execution of the activity.

each entry in the index requires another I/O unless the page being sought happens to be already in the buffer.

The probability of a page already being in the buffer area is the result of a combination of factors—the number of buffers that are available, the usage of those buffers, the amount of time a page has already been in the buffer area, the algorithms used to determine buffer management, and other factors.

In general, under a normally (or fully!) loaded system, a high degree of random buffer hits cannot be anticipated. Consequently, the I/Os required to service a data base query using an index is fairly high.

Now consider system activities not using an index. The mathematics are fairly straightforward. One I/O is required for every page of data. As long as there are not many pages of data, simply accessing every page may be more efficient. When there are many pages of data and when only a few occurrences of data satisfy the search criteria, then using an index is more efficient.

NONSTANDARD EDIT ROUTINES

An option the designer has is to use edit routines for such things as data compression, data encoding, and data encryption. Although these routines can be useful and in some cases save much space (and generally don't cost I/O), the designer must keep in mind that every access of data, update of data, and so forth incurs the penalty of CPU overhead. Figure 4.15 illustrates the difference between using edit routines and not using them.

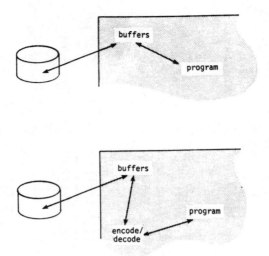

Figure 4.15 (*a*). Data access without edit routines; (*b*). data access in the face of edit routines.

As long as there are a minimal number of edit routines in use, the overhead may not be a major consideration. However, when edit routines are used frequently, the CPU overhead can mount.

ROW SIZE GREATER THAN 4K BYTES

The defined length of a row, if greater than 4k bytes, will cause the table to be processed in the 32k-byte buffer area, thus damaging performance, as shown in Figure 4.16.

The defined length of a fixed-length row is simply the bytes used by the columns (collectively), plus overhead bytes. The defined length of a variable-length row (that is, a row that contains one or more variable columns) is the maximum length of the variable columns, plus the overhead of the fixed-length columns.

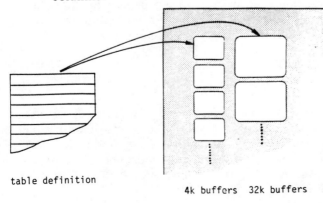

table definition

4k buffers   32k buffers

Figure 4.16 The definition of a table determines in which buffer pool the table will be processed.

In actuality a variable-length row may never occupy all its defined space, but the DB2 space management algorithm manages the data as if every row used the maximum amount of data.

As new releases of DB2 occur, the data base designer needs to keep abreast of the changes, as future changes and improvements at the detailed level will have a major impact on performance.

CHAPTER 5
THE DB2 BATCH ENVIRONMENT

The first consideration of the production environment is online performance and availability. When adequate online performance cannot be achieved, the question must be asked, Why do transaction processing at all?

There is more to the production environment than online peak-period processing. The other major production environment is the batch environment, which typically occurs during after peak-period processing hours. Even though the DB2 set processing orientation is ideal for batch sequential processing, there are several aspects to the batch environment that must be carefully considered.

THE BATCH WINDOW

The peak-period processing time frame usually defines—by default—the batch window. In short, everything that is not peak period is considered to be the batch window. The batch window then is that period of time when system resources can be used with no impact on online performance. Typically, long sequential processes are run in the batch window.

It is very important that the batch window be carefully estimated and the batch window time frame be formally defined.

As long as a shop handles a small amount of processing and/or a small amount of data, then the batch window will probably remain adequate for all the batch needs in the foreseeable future. Faced with large amounts of processing and/or large amounts of data (as is common in the production environment), however, the batch window on occasion may not be adequate. Over time, the batch window tends to shrink. When the batch window becomes inadequate, the computer operator is left with Hobson's choice—either run the online environment in a performance-impaired state, or do not do some amount of batch processing. In either case, the end user suffers. Consequently, when the production environment is being planned, more than casual attention should be paid to the batch window.

To determine if all batch processing will fit in the window, a series of crude measurements can be made. The following example illustrates one of these crude measurements.

Suppose a large data base, with 10,000 pages of data, must be scanned. Assume the index will not be used, and assume that the data is reasonably well organized.

Assume that no other program will attempt to access the data while the scan is occurring. To calculate the length of the batch run, two times are calculated: initiation and shutdown time and data base processing time. (Note that machine time, not elapsed time, is being calculated here.)

Processing time = initiation and shutdown + data base processing.

Now data base processing time must be calculated. In general, each page of data will require around 25 milliseconds for the I/O needed.

Data base processing = 10,000 pages × 25/1000 seconds.

Now assume that 30 seconds of startup and shutdown time are required.

Processing time = 30 secs + (10,000 × 25/1000) = 280 seconds = 4.66 min.

Many other factors beyond just machine requirements must be considered in the calculation of total batch resources required.

- Does the data base have to be scanned sequentially? If it can be scanned in parallel, then elapsed time may be substantially less than machine time.
- How busy is the machine? Does the machine have to process a heavy workload and consequently stretch elapsed time significantly longer than machine time?
- What contention will there be for data? If there is a fair amount of contention for data, elapsed time may be significantly longer than machine time.

In short, the simple calculation presented for machine time requirements gives only a relative figure for the rough estimation of the required length of the batch window.

WHAT RUNS IN THE BATCH WINDOW

The sorts of activities that typically run in the batch window include

- utilities, including backup, image copies, space management, data analysis, reorganization of data, and data definition.
- applications, such as sorting, merging, summarization, and extraction.
- system software for testing, release preparation, and the like.

All of the processing requirements for the batch window must be factored into total batch window requirements, but many of the processes that are run are only incidental to the application designer. For example, the designer has very little influence over the data analysis utilities that are run by data administration and data base administration. However, the designer does have influence over such batch activities as the batch application processing that occurs and the size of the data bases. As a consequence, this chapter will focus on those aspects that can be controlled by the designer.

I/O AND JOINED DATA BASES

In the online environment, data bases that require joins use much I/O and in doing so potentially harm performance. Joined data bases can be detrimental to the amount of resources used in the batch window as well as the online window. Careless or uninformed usage of joined data bases can cause massive amounts of I/O to be consumed. The tremendous savings of I/O that is possible is illustrated by an example. Consider the data structure found in Figure 5.1.

The three data in Figure 5.1 are a parts data base, a supplier data base, and a parts-supplier cross-reference data base. The intent of processing for the batch program being considered is to create records for each part-supplier relationship for the two data bases—a classical batch sequential processing activity.

PARTNO	DESCR	UM	QOH
01258-QX	ball bearingbox	900	
01258-QZ	plate	unit	89
01260	assem 18	crat	125
01268	assem 980	unit	0
:	:	:	:

PARTNO/SUPP	
01258	JONE
01258	KANS
01258	EMPO
01259	JONE
:	:

SUPPLIER	NAME	PHONE
JONES Hdware	JP Carson	998-0791
KANSas SupplyJB	Rivers	807-7760
EMPOrium	R D'field	880-8076
WILSon SupplyB	Hackett	908-5554

data base statistics:

PARTNO Table	-	40 rows/page	250 pages	10000 parts	
PART/SUPP Table	-	150 rows/page	200 pages	30000 part/supp xrefs	
SUPPLIER Table	-	25 rows/page	40 pages	1000 suppliers	

Figure 5.1

A simple approach is to use a relational join of the two data bases to be scanned and simply create the intersection of the two data bases. The relational join would begin with the parts data base and select a part. Then the cross-reference data base would be accessed, based upon the value of the part, and select all the suppliers that supply the part. Then the different suppliers would be accessed, completing the join.

This simple programming technique creates the call pattern shown by Figure 5.2.

Figure 5.2 shows that the parts data base is accessed sequentially, and the pattern of access previously suggested is followed.

The amount of I/O used to process the simple algorithm is considerable. Indeed, just how much I/O is consumed?

The parts data base is scanned sequentially using 250 I/Os (assuming buffer flushing does not occur). The parts supplier data base is likewise scanned sequentially using another 200 I/Os (and likewise assuming buffers are not being rapidly flushed). Then each entry into the supplier data base goes into a different page (excepting the occasional fortuitous buffer hit) using 30,000 I/Os. (For the sake of argument, assume 27,000 actual I/Os are done at a rate of 10 percent fortuitous buffer hits). The number of I/Os needed to process the simple batch join are

$$250 + 200 + 27,000 = 27,450 \text{ I/Os}$$

Now consider a much more complex programming approach. Assume that the part-supplier relationship is sorted and is ordered by supplier order. Next the sorted part-supplier data is passed against the supplier data base, creating a part/supp/supplier intermediate record. Now the part/supp/supplier intermediate records are sorted by part number, and the parts data base is scanned and matched against the part/supp/supplier intermediate record, creating the desired part-supplier joined data.

Consider the I/O required to support this algorithm.

part1	part1/suppA	supplier A
	part1/suppG	supplier G
	part1/suppL	supplier L
part2	part2/suppB	supplier B
	part2/suppC	supplier C
	part2/suppG	supplier G
	part2/suppM	supplier M
	part2/suppP	supplier P
part3	part3/suppA	supplier A
part4	part4/suppC	supplier C
	part4/suppK	supplier K
	part4/suppL	supplier L
:	:	:

Figure 5.2 Call sequence to join the two data bases.

1. Sort part/supp into supplier order—200 reads, 200 writes, sort I/O
2. Creation of part/supp/supplier intermediate records—200 reads (part-supply sorted data), 40 reads (supplier data), 200 writes (of the intermediate records, assuming the intermediate record fits into the same number of pages as read out of)
3. Sort intermediate records by part number—200 reads, 200 writes, sort I/O
4. Merging of intermediate record with parts data—250 reads, 200 reads, 400 writes (assuming the joined record created is long enough to require more space)

The I/O required then is

step 1	400 I/Os	sort I/Os
step 2	440 I/Os	
step 3	400 I/Os	sort I/Os
step 4	850 I/Os	
total	2090 I/Os	2 sort I/Os

Even if the sorts require as much as 1,000 I/Os (which is likely too high a number), the economics of not using the simple relational join greatly favors a less straightforward approach of sorting and merging data.

The order of magnitude of difference in I/Os used is anything but farfetched, and the I/Os consumed in the batch environment are as important as the I/Os in the online environment when they are considered collectively for the batch window.

Furthermore, the example shown is for relatively small amounts of data over very simple relationships which use indexed, clustered data—the best of all possible worlds. In something less than the best of all worlds, it is safe to say that the I/O consumed by the first approach would be substantially more.

Consequently, the designer must be very careful in the design and management of joined relationships in the batch environment.

PARALLEL SEQUENTIAL RUNS

An important design strategy in the management of the batch window is the ability to break long batch processes into a series of shorter-running processes that can be run in parallel. Consider the two types of runs shown in Figure 5.3.

There are two scenarios in Figure 5.3. In one scenario all parts are updated in a single batch run, requiring four hours of processing. In another scenario each batch run updates a quarter of the data base, and an elapsed time of one hour is required. In addition, the runs can be run on separate processors.

The ability to break large runs into asynchronously executable shorter runs depends upon many factors, such as

- the ability to insulate data. If all four shorter runs operated on the same data, then there would be no point in breaking up the runs.

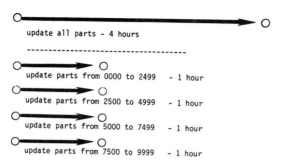

Figure 5.3   Breaking up long runs into a series of shorter runs.

- the ability of the host processor to multiprocess. If only one task can be run at a time, then there is no point in breaking up long batch runs into shorter runs. Often the ability to multiprocess is not a function of the operating system but of the application. Because of the contention for data and the need to run a job serially, classical multiprocessing at the operating system level is not applicable.

The design option that greatly facilitates these goals is the physical separation of data at the application level. When the application divides the data over four physically separate data bases

- update contention is minimized because the system considers the data bases to be separate and distinct
- the ability to spread processing physically over multiple processors is enhanced because data can be processed independently

Of course, when the designer breaks data into physically smaller and separate data bases, then the processing strategy naturally follows. For example, if a data base were broken by geographic location, the batch processing would not be broken along the lines of marketing divisions. In other words, the major divisions of data must apply throughout the organization.

SINGLE EXTRACT PROCESSING

It is common during the batch window to do a certain amount of extract processing. In some cases there is only a small amount to be done; in other cases, a large amount needs to be done. When there is a large amount of extract processing to be done, it makes sense to process against the data being extracted once, not multiple times, as shown in Figure 5.4.

The first savings in the consolidation of extract processing is in the data base that is being extracted: the data base is passed once, not multiple times. Suppose there are m pages of data in the data base being extracted, and suppose there are n extracts of the data base being made. Then the savings is

$$(n - 1) \times m = \text{saved I/O}$$

Saved I/O is not the only performance gain. When extracts are done sequentially, the access to the data base being extracted can become its own bottleneck. In

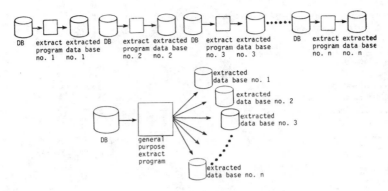

Figure 5.4

other words, extract *n* (and all the processes that depend upon extract *n* being completed) cannot proceed until extracts 1, 2, 3, . . . , *n* − 1 have been completed. When there is a single extract, extract *n* does not have to wait on other extracts to be completed.

To this end the following practices apply:

- Save extracted files until the next extract is run. If unanticipated needs arise, the extracted file may suffice without having to rerun the extract program.

- Extract the full set of information that possibly may be used. Oftentimes an extract is done, and later it is determined that a slightly different set of data is needed. When the extract is done precisely, yielding only the exact amount of data needed, another extract must be done, but when a superset of data is extracted originally, there may be no need to go back and re-extract from the original data base.

SORTING TRANSACTIONS INTO PRIMARY PROCESSING SEQUENCE

A considerable amount of I/O can be saved by sorting the transactions that will be processed in batch into a sequence compatible with the file against which they will be processed. For example, suppose a parts data base is updated nightly in the batch window by transactions collected throughout the day. Suppose 1,000 transactions are gathered on the average, and that the transactions must go against 500 pages of parts data. If the transactions are not sorted into parts sequence, then it is likely that each transaction is going to require its own individual I/O into the parts data base (ignoring the occasional fortuitous buffer hit). In the case where unsorted transactions are processed, 1,000 I/O will be needed.

Now suppose the transaction file is sorted into a sequence compatible with the parts data base. In this case up to 500 I/Os will be required (plus a few more I/Os where the buffer is flushed and must be reread.) The savings in I/O are obvious.

Ordering Batch Runs

Two factors determine the order in which batch runs are executed in the batch window

- the mandatory sequence of execution
- the priority of execution when there is no mandatory order

The mandatory sequence of execution is determined when one job cannot execute until another job is finished. For example, suppose job A updates a data base and job B writes a report from the data base. It does not make sense to run job B until job A has completed. The entire job stream executed in the batch window must be sensitive to this mandatory ordering of jobs.

Not all jobs or job streams are sensitive to a mandatory ordering of processing. When there is no mandatory ordering of jobs, a prioritization of job processing must be made. The sooner in the batch window a job can execute, the less chance the window will close without having executed the job. As a consequence, the most important jobs should be scheduled for execution at the beginning of the batch window.

A normal part of every job (and jobstream) is a contingency plan for the job in the event the job fails to execute. In some cases the job may not run because of an application failure. In other cases the job may not run because of the abnormal closing of the batch window. In any case, every batch job requires its own contingency plan.

In some cases a report will not be delivered to the user, with no other impact. In other cases the impact is more severe. The user may not be able to use the data base until the batch processing is done. At the very least, the contingency plan should outline what other batch (and online) processing will be impacted by a failure to execute.

CONSOLIDATION OF UPDATE REQUIREMENTS

Just as extract requirements should be consolidated into a single program, so should batch update requirements be consolidated, as shown by Figure 5.5.

PEAK-PERIOD PROCESSING

The batch window typically has its peak-period processing moments just like the online window. The consequences of not anticipating peak-period requirements in the batch window can be as severe as not anticipating them in the online window.

When the batch window must be extended, either the online window does not come up as scheduled, or the amount of work done in the batch window is shortchanged.

The peak periods for the batch window typically include month-end processing, year-end processing, and business cycle peak periods. It is worth the DB2 designer's time to anticipate these peak periods.

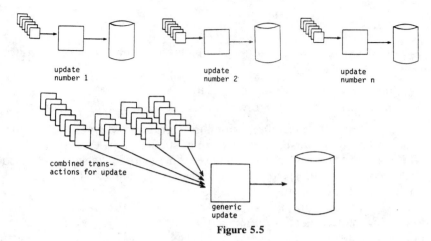

update
number 1

update
number 2

update
number n

combined trans-
actions for update

generic
update

Figure 5.5

When peak periods are anticipated, there are several options the designer has

- split processing (if possible) across more than one processor
- reduce peak periods by altering applications. For example, a bank may produce statements for its customers once a month, but may do so in independent cycles so that on any given working day only a fraction of the customers have statements produced.

SMALL DATA BASES

In many other contexts, the usefulness of small data bases has been noted. In the management of the batch window, small data bases are likewise quite useful. If there is a generic design practice in DB2 for the management of the batch window, it is that data bases be kept as small as possible.

Small data bases

- allow the largest amount of freedom in the structuring of the jobstream in the batch window
- affect (beneficially) not just application batch processing but utilities as well
- give the operator managing the batch window the most flexibility in ending or extending the batch window
- reduce the amount of work needed in reprocessing and/or backing out data in a recovery, in the eventuality of a failure
- automatically reduce the set size that is processed by a DB2 SQL statement
- provide opportunities for parallel processing on separate processors
- can be tailored to a specific user's needs rather than having to fit a large population of users generically

In short, the advantages of small data bases far outweigh the disadvantages, and small data bases are strongly advised for the management of the batch window.

SYSTEM CONSIDERATIONS

In the batch environment, certain standard design practices must be followed. For example, internal data integrity resources must periodically be released, as well as buffers and the like. In the DB2 IMS environment, this means that BMPs must be checkpointed frequently. Periodic checkpoints have the effect of streamlining the flow of processing through DB2.

Checkpointing can be done on a basis of elapsed time, number of calls issued, application logic breaks, or some combination of these.

Summary

The batch environment for DB2 is as important as the online environment. If batch processing extends into the online processing day, the performance implications are obvious.

Planning for the batch window begins with an estimation of how long the window needs to be open, both on the average and in the worst case. The requirements of the batch window are compared with the business requirements of the online day.

Some techniques for the minimization or streamlining of processing in the batch window are

- minimizing the need for relational joins. Usually relational joins require many more resources than simple sorts and merges.
- creating parallel runs. The elapsed time can be significantly shrunk when a long run can be broken into a series of shorter runs that can be run in parallel.
- doing extract processing in a single run.
- sorting transactions in an order compatible with the physical organization of the data base against which the transaction will be run.

CHAPTER 6
DATA STRUCTURES AND DATA RELATIONSHIPS

This chapter is about data relationships and data structures in DB2. The first part of the chapter describes some simple data relationships and where they might be used. The second part of the chapter describes relatively more complex relationships and their usage. Throughout, the emphasis is on the utility and the performance of data relationships.

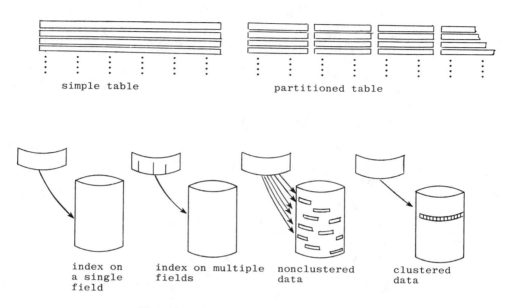

Figure 6.1 The standard DB2 data structures.

STANDARD DATA STRUCTURES

The subject of data structures in DB2 must begin with the standard DB2 structures. DB2 has tables and indexes. Tables can be simple or partitioned. Indexes can exist for single fields or for multiple fields. Indexes can be used for clustered or nonclustered tables. Indexes can be used to force uniqueness in a table. Figure 6.1 shows the standard data structures in DB2.

This short list of the standard DB2 structures belies the richness of structure that can be achieved at the application level.

APPLICATION-SUPPORTED RELATIONSHIPS

The simplest application-supported data relationship in DB2 is from one row in a table to another row in another table. Suppose there are two tables: a part table and a supplier table as shown in Figure 6.2.

Each row in the part table has a supplier field. If all the user desires is to see the supplier of the part, then there is no need to go beyond the part table because

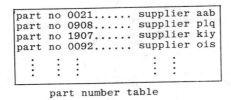
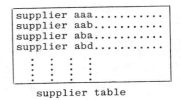

Figure 6.2   The part number and the supplier table share a common field.

the supplier is contained in that table. Suppose that upon having retrieved the part row and having looked at the supplier, further information about the supplier is desired.

The programmer uses the supplier field found in the part table to locate the corresponding row in the supplier table. In the supplier table is much information about the supplier that is not found in the part table. The SQL program shown retrieves some supplier information—NAME and ADDRESS—from the supplier table as shown

```
SELECT NAME ADDRESS
FROM SUPPLIER.TABLE
WHERE SUPP = PART.SUPP
```

Going from part to supplier for a small table is not difficult as long as there are not many suppliers. If there are more than a few suppliers, however, then creating an index on suppliers will allow the entry into the supplier table to be made efficiently.

Now suppose the reverse traversal of tables needs to be made. In this case the programmer is at a supplier row and wishes to see what parts are supplied by the supplier. A SQL request that looks for a parts description is issued.

```
SELECT PART DESCR
FROM PART.TABLE
WHERE PART.SUPP = SUPP
```

In this case there are potentially many parts that are returned as a result of the query. The set of all parts that are supplied is returned. If there are only a few parts, a direct scan of the pages where the parts reside is efficient; if there are many parts, an index into the parts data base using the field supplier will speed up the access of the data. Of course, if there are many parts, then an index will be mandatory.

Although the SQL requests may look very similar, the results are very different. To retrieve a specific part from a supplier requires that one of two things be done. One choice is to leave the data the way it is, retrieve all parts supplied, and look back through the set of parts retrieved for the one being sought. The other choice is to restructure the data, as shown in Figure 6.3.

In the figure a part is shown having a relationship to a supplier in the supplier table. The SQL looking for description and unit of measure call would complete the supplier to part relationship.

```
part no 0021...... supplier aab        supplier aaa........ part no 1097
part no 0908...... supplier plq        supplier aab........ part no 0802
part no 1907...... supplier kly        supplier aba........ part no 0082
part no 0092...... supplier ois        supplier abd........ part no 2297
    :    :    :          :    :    :        :    :    :          :    :    :
    :    :    :          :    :    :        :    :    :          :    :    :
    :    :    :          :    :    :        :    :    :          :    :    :

      part number table                          supplier table
```

Figure 6.3 The part number and the supplier tables share multiple common fields.

```
SELECT PART DESCR UM
FROM PART.TABLE
WHERE PART = SUPP. PART
```

In this case only one part will be returned as a result of the SQL call, but only in the oddest of circumstances would a supplier be the source for a single part. Usually a supplier will be the source for multiple parts. Moreover, only under odd circumstances would a part have one and only one supplier. Under normal circumstances, a part would have multiple suppliers. The data structures that have been shown are ill equipped to handle the more general case of the *m:n* part-supplier relationship.

Consider a data relationship in which a part can have multiple suppliers and vice versa, as shown in Figure 6.4. There are two base tables: a part table and a supplier table. Then there is a cross-reference table from part to supplier and another cross-reference table from supplier to part. A part can have multiple suppliers and vice versa. The SQL call looking for the name and address of a supplier would access the set of suppliers for the part 'xxx. . .' by the call

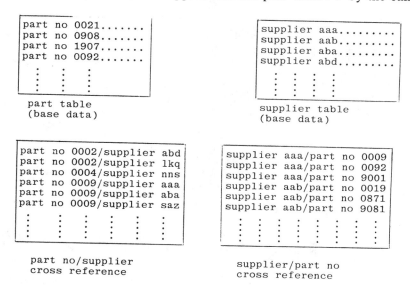

```
part no 0021.......        supplier aaa.........
part no 0908.......        supplier aab.........
part no 1907.......        supplier aba.........
part no 0092.......        supplier abd.........
    :    :    :                :    :    :
    :    :    :                :    :    :
    :    :    :                :    :    :

   part table                   supplier table
   (base data)                  (base data)


part no 0002/supplier abd      supplier aaa/part no 0009
part no 0002/supplier lkq      supplier aaa/part no 0092
part no 0004/supplier nns      supplier aaa/part no 9001
part no 0009/supplier aaa      supplier aab/part no 0019
part no 0009/supplier aba      supplier aab/part no 0871
part no 0009/supplier saz      supplier aab/part no 9081
    :    :    :    :                :    :    :    :    :
    :    :    :    :                :    :    :    :    :
    :    :    :    :                :    :    :    :    :

   part no/supplier              supplier/part no
   cross reference               cross reference
```

Figure 6.4 The part number and supplier base tables and their associated cross-reference tables that support an *m:n* relationship.

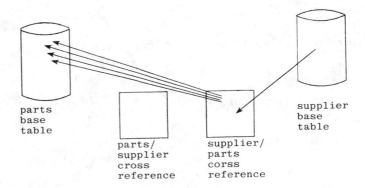

Figure 6.5

```
SELECT SUPPLIER NAME ADDRESS
FROM PART.SUPP.XREF
WHERE PART = 'xxx. . .'
```

Based on the results of the call, the set of suppliers can be accessed to find the information desired.

The cross-reference tables can be used to relate suppliers to parts. The SQL call that looks for the description of a part shown does exactly that.

```
SELECT PART DESCR
FROM PART.SUPP.XREF
WHERE SUPP = 'xxx. . .'
```

Although this call will execute, it will be inefficient because the entire index—the entire cross-reference—must be searched. A more efficient means of access from supplier to part is use of the reverse cross-reference table—the supplier-part cross-reference, as shown in Fig. 6.5.

The contents of the supplier-part cross-reference is the same as the contents of the part-supplier cross-reference. The difference is that the order of the contents are different. The SQL program shown uses the supplier-parts cross-reference to access parts from a supplier efficiently.

```
SELECT PART NAME DESCR
FROM SUPP.PART.XREF
WHERE SUPP = 'xxx. . .'
```

The efficient traversal from parts to supplier and vice versa can be accomplished by the use of two cross-reference tables. Note, however, that when the update of relationships needs to be done, updates must occur in multiple places. Also note that the data are independently organized and can be processed independently (that is, the cross-reference tables can be processed independently, the parts table can be processed independently, and so forth).

Cross-reference tables may simply contain the information pertaining to the relationship being documented, or cross-reference tables may contain other

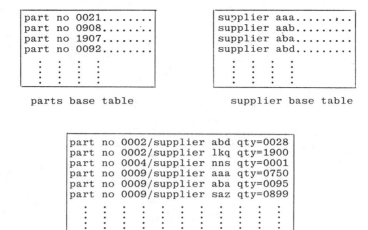

```
part no 0021........          supplier aaa.........
part no 0908........          supplier aab.........
part no 1907........          supplier aba.........
part no 0092........          supplier abd.........
  :    :   :   :                 :    :   :   :
  :    :   :   :                 :    :   :   :
  :    :   :   :                 :    :   :   :

    parts base table            supplier base table
```

```
part no 0002/supplier abd qty=0028
part no 0002/supplier lkq qty=1900
part no 0004/supplier nns qty=0001
part no 0009/supplier aaa qty=0750
part no 0009/supplier aba qty=0095
part no 0009/supplier saz qty=0899
  :   :   :   :   :   :   :   :   :   :   :   :
  :   :   :   :   :   :   :   :   :   :   :   :
  :   :   :   :   :   :   :   :   :   :   :   :
```

Figure 6.6 The field quantity has been added to the parts-supplier cross-reference table.

information as well. That information is often called *intersection information*. For example, for a parts-supplier cross-reference table, the field qty may be added as well, as shown in Figure 6.6.

The field qty (for quantity) indicates the number of parts actually furnished by the supplier. If there are multiple cross-reference tables, intersection data will logically fit in more than one place. In practice, intersection data is stored only in a single place (for most purposes).

MULTIKEYED RELATIONSHIPS

Data relationships can span more than one table. Suppose, in addition to parts and suppliers, orders for parts from a supplier exist as well, as shown in Figure 6.7.

Two tables have to be added. One table shows order number, the supplier to whom the order was made, the date of the order, and the total amount ordered. The second table that has been added shows the order by part, quantity, and price. Relationships now exist between part, supplier, and order. With the tables shown, it is easy to go from order to part or from order to supplier (that is, it is efficient to make such a traversal.)

It is not necessarily efficient to make the reverse traversal. For instance, finding all orders for a part requires traversing the entire order-parts table. The use of a cross-reference would make the part-to-order traversal more efficient. Every time new relationships and new cross-references are added, referential requirements grow, the complexity of the structures grows, and the resource requirements for maintenance grow.

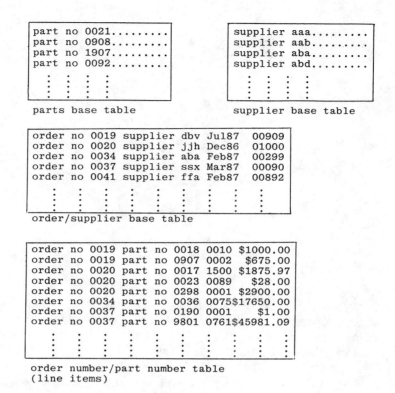

Figure 6.7 Order number data have been added to parts and supplier data.

MULTIKEYED CROSS-REFERENCE TABLES

Cross-reference tables can exist for more than just an *m:n* relationship. For a part, a supplier, and an order, for example, it may be useful to build a table whose key is part, supplier, and order. The table that would result is useful for certain requests.

```
SELECT PART QTY ORDERNO
FROM PART.SUPPLIER.ORDER.XREF
WHERE PART = 'xxx. . .' AND
        SUPPLIER = 'yyy. . .'
```

SECONDARY OR SPARSE INDEXES

Another useful data structure in DB2 that is built at the application level is that of the secondary index or sparse index.

When an index is created in DB2, the index is for all rows. For a large table, there are correspondingly many index entries. If the application developer is

```
acct    date    amt    late
0021   Jul86  167.09  -----
0023   Jul86  209.92  -----
0024   Jul86  187.65  -----
0029   Jul86  175.63  29.78
0031   Jul86   98.80  -----
0034   Jul86  199.00  -----
0036   Jul86  286.98  -----
0037   Jul86  398.73  -----
0038   Jul86  288.39  62.98
0040   Jul86  786.54  -----
0042   Jul86   78.25  -----
0044   Jul86  197.65  -----
0046   Jul86   36.00  -----
0048   Jul86  175.40  -----
0049   Jul86  239.87  43.87
```

```
acct    surcharge
0029     29.78
0038     62.98
0040     43.87
0054     17.74
```

account payment table

Figure 6.8   A sparse index on late paying accounts.

willing to build and maintain separate tables, the size of an index can effectively be reduced. For example, suppose an application processes loan payments. A few loan payments each month have a late surcharge made. If the application were to scan each month's loan payments to determine how many charges there were, many resources would be required. Each entry would need to be scanned.

A better choice would be to build an index and scan the index because an index packs data much more tightly than a row. However, the index would still contain many entries, and most of the entries would indicate no late payment. Even scanning (not to mention building) an index on a large table requires large resources.

A third design option is the sparse index. The sparse index is a table built and maintained at the application level. It contains *only* accounts that have a late payment. The table is simple. It consists of account numbers and possibly the amounts of the surcharges, as shown by Figure 6.8.

For most accounts there is no entry into the sparse index, but when a late surcharge is made, the application inserts a row into the table.

At a later point in time, processing against the sparse index is very efficient. The table, of course, can be indexed and clustered if desired.

The use of a sparse index as an application-maintained data struture can save significant resources, especially in the face of large amounts of data.

INTERNAL ARRAYS

The simple data relationships shown are the common type encountered daily in DB2, but they are hardly the only relationships that are possible. Consider the simple array in Figure 6.9, where activity for an account is posted in the same row as the account.

Up to *n* activities can be posted in a row. Each activity is named in the DB2

acct	date1	amt1	date2	amt2	date3	amt3	......	daten	amtn
0005	860602	234.98	860604	175.00	860606	188.97		860716	675.75
0078	860607	25.00	860607	199.00	860702	67.00		------	------
0086	860604	175.00	------	------	------	------		------	------
0092	860601	25.00	860601	25.00	860603	276.99		860604	25.00
0095	860602	187.65	860603	35.00	860604	50.00		860604	136.92
:	:	:	:	:	:	:		:	:
:	:	:	:	:	:	:		:	:

Figure 6.9 Each row can hold up to *n* occurrences of date and amount activity for an account.

DDL as a different field. Variable-length rows can be created if the number of activities varies widely from one account to the next, or a predetermined number of activities can be allocated for each row if the number of activities is reasonably constant.

The creation of internal tables within a row can save considerable disk space because the key information for the row does not have to be repeated many times. In addition, performance can be enhanced in that only one I/O is needed to retrieve multiple activities for an account. Were the activities for an account defined separately, then the activities might reside in separate pages, thus requiring I/O as the programmer scanned from one activity to the next.

Of course, a burden of complexity is borne at the application level when the usage of internal arrays is specified.

STACKS

Another type of structure that can be made using standard DB2 tools is the *stack*. A stack is useful for first-in, last-out (FILO) processing. A stack is made with a standard DB2 table and a variable that determines where the top of the stack is. Oftentimes this variable is called the *pointer* or the *stack pointer*. The key of the stack indicates the order of entry into the stack.

The creation and use of a stack is illustrated in Figure 6.10. At moment *n* the stack is empty and the variable—the stack pointer—equals zero. At moment *n* + 1 an entry in the stack is made. The first allocation of space in the stack is made (that is, the first row), and the stack pointer is set to one. At moment *n* + 2 the next entry in the stack is allocated, and the stack pointer is set to two At moment *n* + 3 the most recent entry in the stack is removed. Space previously used is freed, and the stack pointer is set to one. At moment *n* + 4 the most current entry in the stack (the only entry) is removed, and the stack pointer is set to zero.

Stacks are useful for recursive processing, such as that found in the bill of materials explosion algorithm. The pointer indicates where the most recent entry into the stack is. When the pointer equals zero, the stack is empty. The stack is normally a table that is defined to DB2 like any other table. The discipline in the usage of the stack is maintained at the application level.

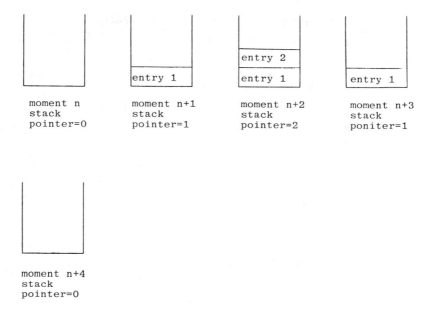

moment n   moment n+1   moment n+2   moment n+3
stack   stack   stack   stack
pointer=0   pointer=1   pointer=2   poniter=1

moment n+4
stack
pointer=0

Figure 6.10   The dynamics of a stack over time as entries are inserted and deleted from the stack.

LOGICALLY RELATED TABLES

Another form of data relationship that is possible in DB2 is the creation of logically related data. In DB2, multiple tables can have the same key or partial key. In that sense, tables are logically related by the common key that they share. Of course, in DB2 the tables can be defined as part of a data base, but DB2 does not participate in the maintenance of the logical key relationships.

The system may or may not know of the relationship between logically related tables. The example shown in Figure 6.11 for suppliers contains four logically related tables: a base table where common information about every supplier exists, a supplier-order table where the contact for any order is stored, the supplier-delivery table where specific delivery information is stored, and the supplier-discount table, where the date of discount, percent, location, and total amount of discount are stored.

Each table contains normalized data. Supplier is the primary key of all of the tables, and some of the tables have more than one key, although no two tables have exactly the same key. The tables logically form a data base. The system may not be aware of the fact that there is a relationship between the different tables. The coordination of update, insert, delete, and so forth must be done at the application level.

suppno	name	addr	phone
0019A	Emporium	123 Grand	555-1908
0019C	Jones Hd	1712 1st St	555-8970
0021	Casper S	760 Main	555-8871
0021D	Wilson	East Drive	889-9802
0021E	Gart Bro	16th St Mall	887-9982
0023	D Cook	SW Plaza	770-9981

supplier base data table

suppno	order	contact
0019A	00325	D Reeves
0019A	00368	J Elway
0019A	00692	S Winder
0019C	00019	S Sewell
0019C	00290	S Sewell
0019C	00498	B Bryan

supplier/order contact table

suppno	deliv addr	deliv contact
0019A	hdqtrs	V Johnson
0019C	hdqtrs	M Jackson
0021	1455 Tincup	G Wilhite
0021D	64 N Ranch	C Kay
0021E	1455 Tincup	G Wilhite
0023	hdqtrs	V Johnson

supplier/delivery table

suppno	discount	terms
0019A	15%	over 100.00
0019A	5%	pymnt on receipt
0019A	2.5%	prepaid
0019C	5%	over 1000.00
0019C	2.5%	prepaid
0021	5%	prepaid
0021D	10%	pymnt on receipt

supplier discount table

Figure 6.11

KEY SPLITTING

The simple data relationships discussed so far are not the only possibilities in DB2. Another common structuring of data is shown in Figure. 6.12.

A supplier-order data base is shown as *n* physical tables. The first table contains supplier-order information for suppliers whose keys begin with 0. The second table shows supplier-order information for suppliers whose keys begin with 1, and so forth. Each of the tables forms logically a single table, even though there are in fact *n* physical tables.

The tables may or may not contain roughly the same amount of data. If table 1 contains 200 suppliers whose key begins with 0 and all other tables contain 75 suppliers in all, then table 1 is likely to have much more data in it than all other tables. If table 2 contains one or two suppliers who have received many orders and the other tables contain information about suppliers who only infrequently

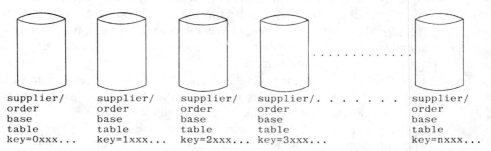

Figure 6.12   Another relationship of data.

receive orders, then table 2 is likely to be proportionately larger than all the other tables.

The simple distribution of data based on key value separation does not necessarily ensure an even split of data, although the key ranges may be divided evenly.

Another aspect of data splitting by key range is that the definition of the data to the system is identical to each table. Each table contains the same key, the same type of data, the same type of data elements, and so forth. In short, the DDL definition is identical. Only the contents of the tables are different. The splitting of data must be accomplished by programs or by standard DB2 partitioning of data. As will be discussed later, splitting data by key range is useful for enhancing system availability, managing large volumes of data (such as that found in an archival environment), and enhancing the performance of data that must be reorganized frequently.

RECURSIVE STRUCTURES

A useful structure supported by DB2 application code is that of the recursive structure. A recursive structure is nothing more than a relationship of a table with itself, rather than with another table. There are two forms of recursive structures: hierarchical recursive structures and peer-level recursive structures. Consider a part number bill of material structure as shown in Figure 6.13.

A part is shown as having one or more subassemblies. The subassembly has its own subassemblies, and so forth. Two DB2 tables represent this hierarchical recursive structure. The base table contains part and nonkey information representing all parts. A second table contains two keys, the assembly and the subassembly.

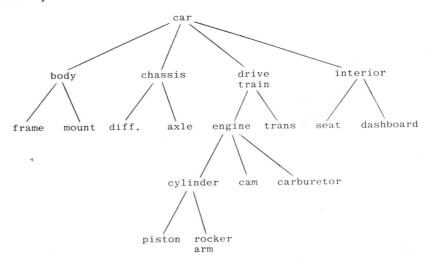

Figure 6.13 A simple bill of material structure for an automobile.

Figure 6.14 Substitute parts for part 1053—a form of peer-level recursion.

The second kind of recursive relationship represented in an application-supported DB2 relationship is the peer-level recursive relationship. In the bill of material example, parts of data related to each other in a hierarchical manner in which one part was a "parent" of another part. In a peer-level recursive relationship, all nodes or components of the recursive structure are peers. For example, in the manufacturing environment, a part may have one or more substitute parts.

Two DB2 tables can be defined to support this peer-level relationship. One table is the base table, as previously described. The other table is the substitute part table. The substitute part table contains two keys, the part and its substitute. A chain of substitute parts can be created by going from a part to its substitute, to the substitute's substitute, and so forth. There is no notion of a hierarchy of parts as there was in the bill of material structure.

SUMMARY

This chapter has discussed some simple and advanced data structures and relationships that can be built in DB2. The structures have been described along with salient points of usage. The simple tables of DB2 can be creatively extended to form elegant structures.

CHAPTER 7
REFERENTIAL INTEGRITY

Referential integrity is the action taken by the system or the application to ensure that the integrity of data relationships across tables is complete and valid. In previous discussions data structures and relationships were addressed. Referential integrity is the means by which those data relationships are built and maintained. This chapter identifies what typical forms of referential integrity can be implemented.

APPLICATION RESPONSIBILITY

Through DB2 Release 3, referential integrity is the responsibility of the application designer. Referential integrity is implemented only to the extent that the application designer specifies. Unlike other data base management systems, in DB2 there is no system facility for the support of referential integrity.

Consider the simple relationship between a part and a supplier as shown in Figure 7.1. A part is provided by a supplier, and a supplier provides a part. There may be multiple parts for a supplier or multiple suppliers for a part. The most straightforward way to represent the $m:n$ part-supplier relationship is through a cross-reference relationship. To support the cross-reference relationship, two cross-reference tables exist: a part-supplier cross-reference table and a supplier-part cross-reference table.

The contents of the two cross-reference tables are identical—only the order of the contents is changed. (In other words, any relationship supported in one cross-reference table will be supported in the other cross-reference table.)

The dynamics of the tables are illustrated by an example. On day 1 part A is added to the parts data base, and supplier B is added to the supplier data base. At this point in time, there is no relationship between the part and the supplier, even though the base information is in the system. On day 2 the production control analyst decides that part A can have supplier B as a provider. At that time two entries are made into the cross-reference tables.

In the part-supplier cross-reference table, a row is inserted with keys: part A, supplier B. In the supplier-part cross-reference table a row is inserted: supplier B, part A.

At this point in time, a relationship exists between part A and supplier B. Upon termination of the relationship, both entries in the cross-reference tables need to be deleted. Note that the termination of the relationship does not necessarily mean the termination of the base data. Part A can go on existing as well as supplier B. It's just that they no longer have a relationship.

Of course, if part A is deleted or if supplier B is deleted, then at that moment the relationship between the two is likewise deleted.

Figure 7.1 An $m:n$ part-supplier relationship.

DIFFERENT FORMS OF REFERENTIAL INTEGRITY

This simple form of a data relationship supported by referential integrity serves to illustrate the basic interactions. There can be *many* forms of referential integrity over different types of relationships. As an example of a simple form of referential integrity, if employee payroll status equals "a" for active, then employee death date must equal null values. As another simple example of a data relationship, if employee row does not exist, then an employee dependent row must likewise not exist. The types of referential integrity and data relationships take many forms. The forms taken are patterned after the business rules of an enterprise.

Referential integrity is an application design and implementation issue primarily during the data base activities of insertion and deletion of data. As data is inserted and deleted, it must conform to the basic existence dependency rules of the business or enterprise. On occasion, replacement of data (that is, update of data) will affect the activities of referential integrity.

The amount of work caused by referential integrity can be significant. For example, suppose in a manufacturing environment a supplier is deleted. With the deletion of a supplier comes a deletion of all orders to the supplier, all part-supplier and supplier-part relationships, and so forth, as shown in Figure 7.2. The amount of data accessed and the number of deletions done can be enormous.

One scenario for the maintenance of the relationship is for maintenance to occur immediately upon changing of the data. For example, in the case of the manufacturing environment, when a supplier is deleted, the deletion of all related supplier information is done in the execution of the same program in which the supplier was deleted. The effect is continuous integrity of the data relationship.

Oftentimes, maintaining referential integrity is quite expensive in terms of the resources consumed on behalf of integrity. In the case of a deletion of a supplier, many I/Os may be consumed by the subsequent deletion of related supplier data and data relationships.

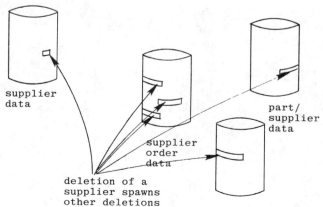

supplier
data

part/
supplier
data

supplier
order
data

deletion of a
supplier spawns
other deletions

Figure 7.2

DEFERRED REFERENTIAL INTEGRITY

Because of the online resources consumed, instantaneous maintenance of referential integrity often is not desirable or even possible. An alternative strategy is to do data base updates, deletions, and inserts online and leave the maintenance of relationships for later batch processing. This strategy saves online resources in that heavy maintenance occurs away from the online window.

However, the deferred maintenance approach to referential integrity has an exposure. From the time that the online update is made until the batch maintenance of the relationship is done, the data is logically impure. In other words, for a period of time the integrity of the relationship has been violated.

Depending upon the data and the nature of the relationship that is supported by referential integrity, this exposure may or may not be significant. If the exposure is serious, then a strategy of deferred maintenance will not suffice.

There may be other economies in delaying the maintenance and verification of referential integrity. Consider the example of an order, a part, and a supplier. These entities are logically related by the business of the enterprise. Suppose that during the daytime the orders are received. Each order normally contains many line items. To verify that an order can be filled during the daytime requires verifying the existence of the supplier and the part, as well as other related items. For the verification of a large order, many I/Os are required.

Suppose orders are stored during the day with no verification. During the evening all daily orders are batched together and the parts that have been ordered are sorted in part sequence. Now when the existence of a part must be verified, it will be verified only once, not each time it was ordered during the day.

For example, if throughout the day there have been ten orders for part ABC, then the verification of the existence of part ABC will be done only once in the evening, not ten times throughout the day, as illustrated by Figure 7.3.

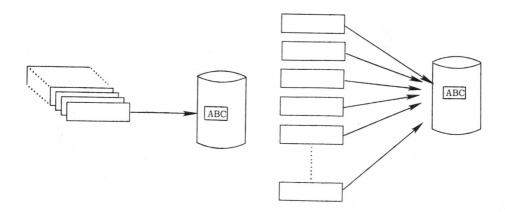

Figure 7.3   When transactions are batched and verification is deferred until the end of the day, only a single verification need be done.

The result is that the batching and sorting of post online activities can be much more efficient than handling the same activity individually throughout the day. Of course, an order must wait for overnight verification to determine if it was a valid order, which may not be acceptable to the customer in some cases.

Consider the case when an order appears that contains one or more invalid parts. The part (or line item) is deleted and the order is adjusted. Depending on the customer and the order, the customer may or may not be notified that the part being ordered will not be filled.

APPLICATION CONVENTIONS

Another way that significant savings can be made in the implementation of referential integrity is in the usage of application conventions. An application convention is merely a means of coordinating the needs for referential integrity over an entire application. Application conventions apply where one data relationship is known to be dependent on other relationships. For example, suppose a delivery is made of a part to a customer based on an order.

The application programmer needs only verify that an order for a part has occurred. Referential integrity does not need to confirm the existence of the part itself, based on the assumption that an order for a part could not exist unless earlier application code had made the verification. The total needs for referential integrity can be limited by carefully coordinating the different applications that operate on data.

INDEPENDENT AUDITS

A final concern of referential integrity is the occasional audit that needs to be made, independent of the normal application code that supports updates, deletions, and insertions. In theory, as long as a relationship is designed and programmed correctly, there is no need for an independent audit of data relationships. However, design and programming flaws do exist, as do operating flaws. There is a host of reasons why data relationships—under the best of circumstances—sometimes get out of synchronization.

As a result, independent audits created by the application programmer need to be run periodically. Consider the audit of a simple part, supplier, part-supplier cross reference, and supplier-part cross reference. An audit program can be written to capture all the parts (from the part table) and sort them if necessary. The first step of the audit matches the sorted parts against the part-supplier cross-reference. Every cross reference entry should have a corresponding part entry, although not every part will necessarily be found in the part-supplier cross-reference. Next the supplier table is sorted on supplier number (if necessary) and is matched against the supplier-part cross-reference table. Like the part and part-supplier cross reference, every entry in the supplier-part cross reference must exist in the sorted supplier table. A supplier may or may not exist in the supplier-part cross reference.

Next one of the cross reference tables is sorted into the sequence of the other one, and the two tables are matched against each other. There will be a one-to-one relationship between the two tables. Any entry existing in one table and not the other will be an error.

FREQUENCY OF AUDIT

The frequency of audit is determined by several factors, such as

- how sensitive the data is
- how complex the relationship is
- how much data is contained in the relationship

Generally speaking, the volume of data that must be manipulated is such that audits are done on as infrequent a basis as possible.

Summary

In summary, this chapter has discussed what referential integrity is, the different levels of complexity of data relationships, and how referential integrity is based on business rules. The issue of when to ensure referential integrity and what application conventions are was discussed next. Finally, the auditing of the relationships was discussed.

CHAPTER 8
DENORMALIZATION

The performance of relational systems can be enhanced through the physical placement of data in an optimal fashion. The result of normalization is usually many small tables of data. When data must be dynamically joined, the result is the consumption of much I/O. There may be significant performance gains to be made by denormalizing the data immediately prior to physical data base design.

Denormalization is the design process of taking normalized data and producing a physical design in which normalized data is rearranged so that optimal access and manipulation of data can be achieved.

NORMALIZATION OF DATA

The process of normalization, which is one of the foundations of relational technology, requires that data be organized into individual tables. Each table is distinct from other tables and has its own unique key. All of the nonkey data in a table logically depends on the full key of the table for its existence. For example, in a table representing an employee, the key of the employee may be employee number, and the nonkey information may include information such as date of hire, location of hire, starting position, and so forth. If an employee did not exist, there would be no date of hire or location of hire. The nonkey data depends on the key data for its existence. Figure 8.1 shows a simple normalized table.

Prior to physical data base design, all data is normalized into relational tables. One result of normalization is that the tables defined tend to have few data elements in each table, and there tend to be many tables. Nothing is inherently wrong with this very fine division of data, but if a high volume of processing is to be done and if the processing requires frequent reference from one table to the next, then the result is the consumption of much I/O. When much I/O is consumed, the result is poor performance. Figure 8.2 illustrates the dynamic joining of several relational tables.

Note that if the high-volume processing goes against only data in a single table, then the techniques of denormalization do not apply. When high-performance processing goes against a single table, then combining tables (that is, denormalizing tables) has little or no effect on performance and the I/O consumed.

employee no	date of hire	location of hire	conditions
0012	850312	Tucson Az	finish degree
0015	701215	El Paso Tx	------------
0018	750730	Tempe Az	------------
0020	761116	Dallas Tx	------------
0022	771215	Houston	no part time work
0024	821217	Waco Tx	complete CPA
0025	791010	Pecos Tx	------------
0028	810801	Las Cruces NM	------------
⋮	⋮	⋮ ⋮	⋮ ⋮

Figure 8.1 A simple normalized table. Each nonkey field depends on the key for its existence.

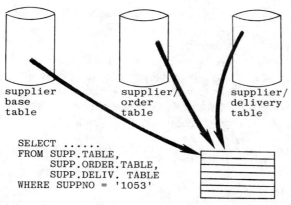

SELECT ......
FROM SUPP.TABLE,
     SUPP.ORDER.TABLE,
     SUPP.DELIV. TABLE
WHERE SUPPNO = '1053'

Figure 8.2 A SQL program executes and dynamically forms a new table based on the values found in existing tables.

Only when processing must frequently jump from one table to the next will denormalization enhance performance. Denormalization will also enhance performance of the offline environment if there is a heavy amount of processing occurring in batch and if the batch processing frequently jumps from one table to the next.

Denormalization, then, is the process of taking many small tables and combining them into fewer, larger tables, so that less I/O is required. Figure 8.3 shows a table that has been denormalized.

The data elements in the same row in Figure 8.3 have different existence criteria and as such are not normalized.

THE USAGE MATRIX

The first step in the denormalization of data is to determine what processes represent the heaviest volume and what tables those processes are operating on. A convenient aid in this analysis is to create a matrix matching process against tables. Going down the left-hand side of the matrix are the tables that are being analyzed. Going across the page are the processes that are being analyzed. Figure 8.4 shows an example of a usage matrix.

employee number	name	address	age	manager	office phone	school	degree
00013	G Frey	123 Main	39	B Bach	555-1234	Yale	MBA
00016	D Henley	1689 1st St	42	B Bach	555-2298	Harvard	MS
00019	T Schmit	134 Grand	43	C B Sag	778-9981	UCLA	BS
00021	J Walsh	990 Teton	45	B Bach	887-3397	USC	BA
00201	D Felder	1455 Tincup	39	W Nelson	889-9972	Stanford	--
00202	S Nicks	220 Pine	41	T Wynett	998-2208	U Texas	BS
00204	M Fleet	220 Pine	45	G Jones	555-6692	U Conn	--

Figure 8.3 An unnormalized table.

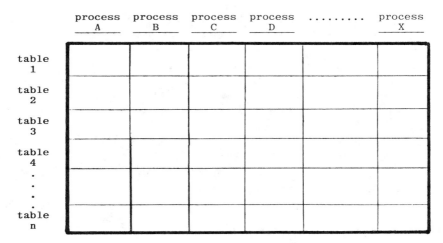

Figure 8.4   The process-table usage matrix.

Each cell in the matrix, then, represents the access of the table by the process.

After the matrix is created, the first, rather raw analysis is to determine how many times the process will be executed, usually for a 24-hour period. (Some period of time must be chosen as a baseline for the building of the table-process matrix.) Then the number of times the process will operate against the table is calculated for every table. For example, if process A accesses tables 2, 5, and 6 and process A executes 100 times a day, then the cell representing the intersection of process A and tables 2, 5, and 6 will contain the value 100, and other cells where the table was not accessed will contain a value of zero.

In addition to the mere access of data, the analyst may wish to use the usage matrix to keep track of update and access information. In other words, it may be useful to distinguish between access and update for some types of processes.

The estimate of the number of executions for a process can become complex because of several factors. In some cases a process has never been run before and the number of times the process will be executed is purely a guess. In other cases the process will execute 100 times on one day and 1,000 times on another day, in a random pattern. One process may require high performance, yet other processes will not need the same level of performance. Still another factor is that a transaction will show an execution frequency of 1,000 and a batch process will show a frequency of execution of 1 or 2 for the same 24-hour period.

THE PROCESSING FREQUENCY ANOMALIES

All of these anomalies need to be taken into account if the denormalization process is to be effective. In the case in which the number of times a process is to execute is not known, generally speaking the highest reasonable estimate should be used. The estimate may come from empirically derived data, or the estimate may be analytically derived. In any case, to err slightly too high is acceptable; to err too low is not acceptable.

In the case of a substantial difference between one day's processing activities and another day's activities, the high-water mark should be used.

In the case of a substantial difference between the priorities of different transactions, the transactions with the higher priorities should be weighted in favor of the more important transactions. The weighting is done by multiplying the number of transactions run per day by a factor of 2 or 3.

All differences have been accounted for with the exception of the difference between batch processing and online processing. For example, the frequency of execution of an online process may be 400 times a day while the frequency of execution of a batch process may be twice a day.

ESTIMATING ROW ACCESS FREQUENCY

After the number of executions have been placed in the appropriate cell in the matrix, the next step is to determine how many rows of the table will be needed by each execution. In other words, when a process accesses a table, how many rows will it normally access?

For example, the value in a cell is 150, indicating that a process will access a table 150 times throughout the day. The next cell has a value of 200. The analysis now requires that the number of accesses be multiplied by the number of rows per access. The first process accesses one row per access and the next process accesses 25 rows per access. Factoring in the number of rows per execution leaves values of 150 and 5,000 in the two cells. The values in the cells are now more representative of the true processing needs of the system.

The number of accesses per execution in some cases is a very straightforward number, and in other cases it is not. For example, if a process accesses five and only five rows per execution, then it is clear that the process frequency for the cell needs to be multiplied by five. For another cell, suppose that the average number of rows accessed is ten, with a standard deviation of 0.5. This means that most executions will use ten rows, and the cell is multiplied by ten. But, suppose the average number of rows accessed per execution is 15, with a standard deviation of 12.5. In this case the number of rows accessed per execution varies widely. As a rule, half the standard deviation should be added to the mean as the factor to be applied to the frequency of execution. In the example being discussed, half of 12.5 is 6.25, which, added to 15, yields 21.25, the factor that should be used.

At this point, batch processing is factored in. A batch process may show only one execution per day, but in executing the batch process accesses 40,000 rows.

HEURISTIC AND ITERATIVE ANALYSIS

The next analytical step is to determine which tables should be combined and which tables should be clustered. The analysis is heuristic and iterative and does not follow any prescriptive path.

account	balance	activity	date
10089	100.00	+25.00	1215
10089	75.00	-25.00	1216
10089	150.00	+50.00	1216
10089	189.36	+39.36	1217
10089	60.36	-120.00	1218
10089	1060.36	+1000.00	1218

the table that results when balance is superimposed on activity. A new balance is created every time there is an activity, and there is much duplication of key data

account	balance	activity 1 date	amount	activity 2 date	amount	....	activity n date	amount
10089	1060.36	1215	+25.00	1216	-25.00		1218	+1000.00
10091	1078.98	1218	-1000.00	1219	+35.00		----	--------
10092	10908.72	1215	+15000.00	1221	-10.00		1221	+12000.00
10092-1	--------	1222	-12000.00	1224	+2798.76		1224	+35997.19
10092-2	--------	1226	+200.00	1226	-566.98		----	--------
10094	187.56	----	--------	----	--------		----	--------

the table that results when activity is superimposed on balance. There are a widely varying number of activities for each account for the same period of time. Some accounts have no activity - such as account 10094 and other accounts have so much activity that more than one row must be used. When more than one row is used - as in the case of account 10092 - application convention is that the active balance is stored in the first occurrence of the account.

Figure 8.5 Two tables that show that, even when data is related, combining the data into the same row can be difficult and may not be advisable.

The first pass at denormalization is to attempt to combine the most heavily used tables. The total row-table usage may be calculated from the table by adding each line to the right. In other words the total number of rows needed for all processing is the sum of all row accesses going across the page. Based upon the total usage numbers, the analyst asks, Which two or more rows can be merged so that data used together is placed in the same row?

Generally speaking, the rows that can be combined share part of a common key. An employee base table, an employee education table, and an employee job history table may be combined, but an employee table and a parts usage table would not be candidates for combination. The first cut at analysis is to identify heavily used tables that are logical candidates for combination. Key commonality is the first clue to the successful combination of data.

However, not all commonly shared keys can be successfully combined. Consider the simple case of a bank balance table and a bank activity table, where activities add up to the current balance. Certainly these tables share a common key and certainly these tables are used together, but the distribution of keys is so dissimilar that the pieces of data are combined only with difficulty. For example, activity may be incorporated into the balance table, but activity is frequently updated and occurs a variable number of times. Figure 8.5 illustrates the difficulties of combining balance and activity rows. Admittedly some savings can be effected, but at a cost of complexity, which is most likely undesirable.

After the candidates that can be merged together are merged, then the savings analysis is done. In the perfect case, table A is accessed 1,000 times, and table B is accessed 5,000 times per day. By combining the tables, all accesses to B will be combined with accesses to A. The total number of accesses to the combined AB is 1,000 in the optimal case.

The advantage of the usage matrix is that it allows different combinations of data to be merged and allows the different economies of consolidation to be measured quantitatively.

Of course, the analyst should carefully consider the full range of design criteria when combining two tables. Such issues as the ability to split the data at a later point in time and the creation of very large tables should be considered along with the performance considerations.

CLUSTERING ANALYSIS

Considered in combination with the consolidation of tables is the issue of whether data should be clustered or not. When the total number of table accesses was calculated, no considerations were given to whether the access was direct or sequential. In *direct access* a single row and only a single row is accessed. In *sequential access* one row after another is accessed in rapid succession. When data is clustered and much sequential processing occurs, then it may be assumed that multiple rows may be read in a single I/O (that is, as many rows as exist in a page). In the analysis of which rows need to be combined, the issue of clustering can be factored in. When a row is assumed to be clustered, the total number of sequential accesses is adjusted to reflect the lessened need for I/O.

AUTOMATED TOOLS

The combination of consolidation of data and clustering that reduces the *total* number of accesses to the data in the system is the optimal plan for denormalization and clustering of data. Because of the number of tables and the combinations that are possible, this phase of denormalization analysis is heuristic and iterative. It often makes sense to use a spreadsheet tool such as LOTUS 1-2-3 as an aid in this phase of analysis. In using an automated tool, not only can different options be documented, but also new options can be calculated rapidly.

As an example of a successful table denormalization, suppose a supplier-order table and an order-supplier line item table have been specified by the data analysis and normalization process. The supplier-order table contains information about who the supplier of an order is, the supplier contact, and name and phone number, as well as conditions of the order. The order-supplier line item table contains information about the line items of an order, the amount of each item ordered, the price, and so forth. Most processes that access one table access the other. Creating a single table allows access to be done in a single I/O, because consolidation forces the data into the same row. Figure 8.6 shows the effect of consolidation.

| supplier | contact | phone | conditions | item 1 | | item 2 | | |
				part	amount price	part	amount	price ·······
10098	P McCartney	555-8891	FOB	110-a	9000 100.00	1998	800	977.00
10100	R Starr	669-2298	COD	1187	16000.00	---	---	---
10100	G Harrison	778-2209	---	1187	15500.00	1998i	10	67.98
10100	J Lennon	550-8873	FOB	22098	20 998.45	---	---	---
10102	M Jagger	887-3398	FOB	110-s	20 776.00	1109	50	998.21
10103	H Nillson	665-9981	COD	1187	16000.00	---	---	---
·····	·····	·····	·····	·····	·····	·····	·····	·····

Figure 8.6 The consolidation of two tables into a single denormalized row.

part	supplier	supplier name	supplier address
1009	10098	Emporium	123 Grand
1009	10199	Grand Auto	17th Street
1009	19087	Wilson Hd	16 N Ranch
1009	20098	Jones Dry	16th St Mall
1010	10098	Emporium	123 Grand
1011	10099	Denver DG	16th St Mall
1011	10200	Denver DG	SW Plaza
⋮	⋮	⋮	⋮

Figure 8.7 A cross-reference table with name and address added.

REDUNDANCY

After the analysis is done, consider another variable—the deliberate introduction of redundancy into the system. To this point the data in the system have been assumed to be nonredundant. The nonredundancy of data optimizes update of data at the expense of access of data. The issue of denormalization now must address the question, Will the deliberate introduction of redundancy into the system significantly reduce the total number of accesses that the system makes?

This analysis is addressed heuristically and iteratively, like the previous analysis. The first clue as to which data elements are candidates for redundant existence comes from the frequency matrix that has been developed. Those tables that are frequently accessed and not frequently updated may contain data that when positioned redundantly in more than one table reduce total access needs. The analyst must keep in mind that the proliferation of data may reduce access needs but increase update needs when the data values change. Generally speaking, only limited amounts of data are deliberately proliferated.

As an example of the selective use of redundancy, suppose there is a parts table, a supplier table, and a cross-reference table. The cross-reference table contains only the key values—part and supplier. When the cross-reference table is used in going from part to supplier, in most cases only the supplier name and address are needed. Other information contained in the supplier table is accessed infrequently. The analyst places supplier name and address in the parts-supplier cross-reference table as nonkey data, as shown by Figure 8.7.

Supplier name and address are not placed in the supplier-parts cross-reference table. Now, when cross-reference needs to be made to the supplier, only the part-supplier cross-reference table must be accessed, saving an access to the supplier table. The analyst must factor into the savings the work required by the system to keep the supplier name and address current in the cross-reference table. The cross-reference table must be updated—potentially in many places—when supplier name and address change. Fortunately, the fields that have been made redundant are stable fields that do not require frequent maintenance.

After the redundancy analysis is done, the analyst adjusts the matrix to reflect the new pattern of access and update of tables.

employee number	pay Jan 15	pay Jan 30	pay Feb 15	pay Feb 28	pay Mar 15	....
0021	1500.00	1500.00	1500.00	1475.00	1500.00	
0023	1789.00	1775.00	1789.00	1775.00	1789.00	
0024	1050.89	1100.00	1050.89	1100.00	1050.89	
0026	998.78	998.78	998.78	996.35	998.78	
0029	767.90	767.90	767.90	659.89	767.90	
0031	1976.98	1976.98	2060.76	2100.00	2060.76	

Figure 8.8   Pay history data with individual pay amounts organized into an array.

INTERNAL ARRAYS

Another technique of denormalization available to the analyst is the specification of internal arrays of data in a row. If a row contains a small number of nonkey data elements, if the data elements are frequently accessed in a sequential manner, if the pattern of access is stable, and if the number of occurrences of nonkey data can be reliably calculated for the key values of a table, then the analyst should consider violating the first form of normalization by placing the elements of data into an array. In an array a row contains multiple occurrences of nonkey data. When the conditions are met, a substantial savings in resources consumed is possible.

As an example of the usage of an array within a row, consider a payroll history file. The logical design specifies that the twice-monthly paycheck be stored individually, but there is no reason why an annual payroll history table cannot be created. The annual table contains twenty-four occurrences—one for each twice monthly paycheck. The order of insertion of the occurrences of data, the number of occurrences for each employee, and the access of the occurrences is very stable. The violation of the first form of normalization yields many performance dividends, not to mention the savings of space in the reduced need for key data. Figure 8.8 shows this form of denormalization.

INTERLEAVING DATA

A final option appropriate to DB2 that is applicable in a few cases is the interleaving of data. *Interleaving* occurs where two tables are stored in the same page(s) of data. Interleaving is not an option for partitioned data. When the probability of access is high, there may be some performance gains by interleaving data. For example, suppose an account balance table and an account activity table are often accessed together, and the designer does not wish to combine the two tables into a single row. The analyst may sort the data together to combine the two tables into the same page based on like key values.

Upon loading the data bases, the data is loaded in a sequence such that like keys from different tables are stored in the same page. The effect is that one I/O services multiple requests for data from different tables.

There are several problems with interleaving. Interleaving cannot be used with partitioned data. Interleaving must be done as data bases are loaded. Once an interleaved data base is updated, there is no guarantee that the data will be properly placed. Finally, a reorganization of data will not restore the proper order of data after update. Instead, interleaved data must be resorted and reloaded.

As an example of the usefulness of interleaving, consider an account balance and account activity data. Sorting the tables by account and then loading like tables into the same page has the effect of placing unlike tables with like data in the same physical proximity. Of course, update of the data destroys the effect of interleaving. Figure 8.9 shows the interleaved data.

acct balance	acct activity	acct activity	acct activity	acct balance	acct activity ....
10029 $45.02	860612 +12.78	860614 −36.90	860615 +100.00	10031 $100.00	860201 +90.56　....

Figure 8.9　Data that have been interleaved in a DB2 page.

OTHER OPTIONS

The design techniques for denormalization to this point have merged data into the same row so that a minimum of I/O is used, once the row is accessed, but merging unlike data together is not the only denormalization technique. Suppose a bank account table is to be created. The key of the table is the account, and nonkey elements include bank balance, domicile, date account opened, and other similar elements. The key—account number—is 16 bytes in length and the nonkey data is 64 bytes in length. Total row space is 80 bytes.

To enhance performance, the table is split into two tables. One table contains the account key and balance. A row in this table is 22 bytes in length. The other table contains the key and all the other nonkey data elements except balance. The length of a row in this table is 74 bytes.

An analysis of the accounts table shows that the frequency of access of the balance data is heavy. Every time an activity against an account is transacted, the balance table is accessed and updated. The remaining account data—domicile, date account opened, and so on—are accessed very infrequently.

By splitting the data into separate tables, the probability of a fortuitous hit in the buffer is raised. In the original design a row was 80 bytes in length. In a fully packed 4k buffer, about 50 rows would fit. In the new design for the balance table, about 180 rows would fit in the buffer. The odds of a fortuitous buffer hit are raised by shrinking the size of the row with the most activity and packing the highly accessed data together so that there is a greater chance of a buffer hit.

This technique of denormalization is a radical departure from other techniques of denormalization that rely on the consolidation of data.

Summary

In summary this chapter has focused on what denormalization is and why it can enhance performance. The building of a usage matrix to determine the effectiveness of denormalization was discussed, as was the heuristic and iterative analysis that centers around the matrix. An automated tool such as a spreadsheet was suggested to create and maintain the matrix. Finally, the deliberate introduction of redundancy into the system was suggested.

CHAPTER 9
BILL OF MATERIAL PROCESSING

A bill of material is a recursive structure in which one node or component of the structure relates to another node or component of the structure. Bill of material processing is important because it occurs so commonly and because recursive processing and data structures, when not designed properly, can become very complex. In addition to the standard techniques, several alternative processing and design approaches are discussed in this chapter.

THE BILL OF MATERIAL

A bill of materials is a special kind of data relationship in which one occurrence of data relates to another occurrence of data. The data relationship is made unique by the facts that the relationship is between data occurrences of the same type and that the relationship is *m:n*. For example, in a manufacturing environment the parts that are to be manufactured are related to each other by the manufacturing process. The final assembly is made up of subassemblies. Each major subassembly is made up of its own subassemblies. The assembly process is broken down into finer levels of detail until a subassembly is made up of raw goods. Figure 9.1 shows a simple bill of material.

These simple data relationships form what is known as a bill of material. A bill of material describes the manufacturing process from raw goods to final assembly.

At first glance there seem to be substantive differences between finished goods, assemblies, and raw goods. However, each type of part—sometimes called a *node* in the bill of material—contains common information such as description, unit of measure, and quantity. Whether a part is finished, assembled, or raw, it is still a part. The only fundamental difference from one part to the next is the relationship between the parts.

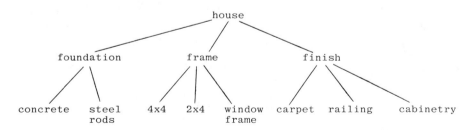

Figure 9.1 A simple bill of material for a house.

RECURSIVE RELATIONSHIPS

The type of relationship in which a part of one type relates to another part of the same type is called a *recursive* relationship. Recursive relationships appear in many places, not just the manufacturing environment. The family tree in which a parent relates to a child is a form of recursion. In the case of the family tree, both

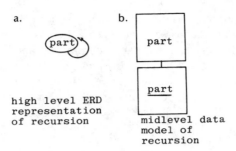

a.

high level ERD
representation
of recursion

b.

part

part

midlevel data
model of
recursion

Figure 9.2 (*a*). High-level ERD representation of recursion; (*b*). midlevel
data model of recursion.

a parent and a child are forms of a human. The typical organization chart is
another classical form of recursion. Each node in the organization chart is a form
of an organizational unit, with one or more relationships to other organizational
units. Recursive relationships are very common, although they are classically
associated with the manufacturing environment.

At first glance there is nothing terribly difficult about recursive relationships.
Nevertheless, processing recursive relationships with relational tables requires
special techniques to keep the design from becoming very complex.

The logical structure used to show recursion is a node pointing into itself,
such as a part pointing to itself in a bill of material or a person pointing to another
as a member of a family tree, as in Figure 9.2.

At the level of physical design—at the DB2 table level—recursive structures
are shown in terms of a base table and one or two pointer tables. The base table
contains information that applies to every part, such as key, description, and unit
of measure. One part table contains the *downward* pointer, and the other pointer
table contains the *upward* pointer. The downward pointer—sometimes called the
where from pointer—contains two fields: the part being pointed at and the part
that is doing the pointing. A typical bill of material structure is shown in Figure
9.3.

In the case of a bill of material, every finished good would have one or more
downward pointers, indicating what subassemblies it was made of. A car would
have a downward pointer for the drive train, for the chassis, for the body, and so
forth. Raw goods would have no downward pointers because they are at the
lowest level of assembly, and nothing goes into raw goods. Subassemblies would
have downward pointers showing what subassemblies they are made of.

a.

part no	desc	u/m	.....
10098	washer	bin	
10099	disc	part	
10201	screw	bin	
10202	bolt	box	
10206	nut	carton	
10209	plate	part	
:	:	:	:

b.

part no/part from	
00012	10097
00012	10098
00012	10201
00012	10207
00013	00459
00013	00896
:	:

c.

part no/part into	
00001	90087
00001	99871
00009	10098
00009	18897
00009	19082
00010	00897
:	:

Figure 9.3 (*a*). parts base data table; (*b*). downward-pointing recursive table; (*c*).
upward-pointing recursive table.

The other type of pointer (that may or may not exist, as will be discussed later) is the upward pointer—sometimes called the *into* pointer. There are two key fields in an upward pointer: the part being pointed at and the part that is doing the pointing. The part that is being pointed at is the lower part of the assembly. For example, a car—an example of finished goods—would have no upward pointers because the car is not assembled into anything else, but raw goods would have many upward pointers because raw goods form the basis for manufacturing.

On occasion the upward pointer contains a nonkey field: quantity. In this case the quantity field indicates the number of subassemblies that go into the next level of assembly. The upward pointer for an engine might contain the value of six for pistons going into an engine, if the engine were a six-cylinder vehicle.

The upward pointer and the downward pointer do not represent different relationships; they are the logical equivalent of each other. However, the upward and downward pointers are used in very different ways. The upward pointer is used to traverse the bill of material structure upward, from raw goods to final product. Conversely, the downward pointer is used to traverse the bill of material structure from the top to the bottom, from the finished product to the raw goods.

If there is never to be a traversal in one direction, then the corresponding set of pointers do not need to be created and maintained. The existence of one set of pointers or the other is a function of the usage of the bill of material structure.

For some bills of material, it is necessary to keep track of the order of subassemblies beneath the assembly. In particular, in DB2 bill of material processing, this sequencing of subassemblies comes in very handy. To achieve this subsequencing, there is another field that needs to be added to the downward pointing table: the *level count* field. Level count is nothing more than the enumeration of the subassemblies of a part at any level. For example, suppose the part 1053 has four parts as its immediate subassembly: 5096, 0012, 1463, and 2007. Part 5096 will have a level count of one, part 0012 will have a level count of two, part 1463 will have a level count of three, and part 2007 will have a level count of four, as shown by Figure 9.4.

When a new part is added as a subassembly for part 1053, it will have a level count of five. Each new part added as a subassembly will have a level count of one greater than the previous part added.

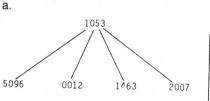

a.

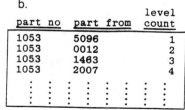

b.

part no	part from	level count
1053	5096	1
1053	0012	2
1053	1463	3
1053	2007	4

Figure 9.4 (*a*). The logical representation of the data structure; (*b*). the part from table after level count has been added.

CONTINUITY OF THE LEVEL COUNT FIELD

When a level count is deleted, the level count sequence must remain intact and continuous. For example, suppose for part 1053 that part 0012 is deleted as a subassembly. When part 0012 is deleted, level count 2 is not present, and the sequence of level counts is broken. There are several options to repair the level count. One option is to set the level count of 9001, the part that was most recently added, to 2, thus resequencing level counts. However, using the last level count fo fill in the level count that was deleted has the effect of resequencing the chain of level counts. The other option that keeps the level counts in sequence and maintains the continuity of the level counts is to resequence all level counts when a deletion is done. If level count n is deleted, then level count $n + 1$, $n + 2$, and so on have their level counts reduced by one. In the case of the deletion of part 1053, when subassembly 0012 is deleted, then the level count for 1463 is set to two and the level count for 2007 is set to three.

In any case, maintaining the continuity of the sequence is the most important factor. Only under unusual circumstances will there be a need to maintain the order of subcomponents of an assembly. In that case it will be necessary to preserve the order through the wholesale resequencing of the level count field when the sequence is interrupted by an insertion or a deletion. In normal cases mixing the order of the subassemblies causes no problem.

A SECOND LEVEL COUNT FIELD

When there are many updates to a bill of material and when the parts that are subassemblies do not have to maintain their original sequence of entry, then it may be worthwhile to store the number of subassemblies at the assembly level. For example, the part 1053 would have a total level count that equaled five, indicating that it had five subassemblies.

When the total number of subassemblies is stored at the assembly level, there are two level counts. One level count indicates how many subassemblies the assembly has, and the other level count indicates the position of the part with its peers.

The management of level counts is unquestionably burdensome and awkward for many bill of material operations. Unfortunately, many bill of material operations depend on the uniqueness forced by level count in the face of set-only processing.

THE GENERALIZED RECURSIVE STRUCTURE

The base table and the one or two sets of pointers constitute what is termed the *generalized* form of recursion. The generalized form of recursion

- provides a generic representation of the key and nonkey data applicable to all nodes in the bill of material structure

- can be used to represent *n* levels of recursion where *n* is a variable number
- has no restrictions as to what type of node can be placed where in the logically derived bill of material structure

Each of the salient aspects of the generalized bill of material structure will be explored.

The definition of every node is identical. A finished good has associated with it a description, unit of measure, quantity, and so forth. All other levels of nodes in the structure have the same nonkey data associated with them. The type of data that is applicable does not change from one node to the next. Of course, the contents of the data vary from one node to the next, but not the form.

There is no limit to the number of levels of recursion that can be represented. To create another level simply requires the formation of a new relationship, which the generalized structure is equipped to do, ad infinitum. To create a new level merely requires creating a new node with the lowest level pointing into the existing structure.

There are no structural implications of the different levels. For example, a common bolt may be a raw good, but the bolt can go into the bill of material assembly in any number of places—into the body of the car or into the engine of the car.

A SIMPLE EXAMPLE

As a simple example of processing against the base tables and the upward and downward pointers, suppose an engineer wished to see the subassemblies for part 1053. The execution of the SQL program produces the desired parts.

```
SELECT PARTFROM DESC
FROM TABLE.DOWN
WHERE PART = '1053'
```

The results of the execution of this SQL program would be all the downward parts (that go down one level) and their descriptions. If all that is required is simple recursive processing, as shown, then there is no problem, and practically any structuring of recursive data would suffice. However, recursive processing can become complicated very quickly where more than one level of recursion is required. For example, suppose the engineer wished to take a part down to its raw goods. Then each part would in turn need its own recursive processing. At this point program logic becomes very complex.

BILL OF MATERIAL EXPLOSION

A standard process associated with bill of material processing is known as the *explosion*. An explosion is the level-by-level expansion of a part into all of its subassemblies, down to the point of raw goods. The SQL program that has been discussed goes down one level of recursion. What is required for an explosion is a similar traversal of the structure down *n* levels.

Managing the complexity of processing in DB2 requires a special data structure known as a *stack*. The stack can be built as a regular DB2 table or can be built in working storage. In the example that is being developed, the stack is built in memory but could just as well have been built as a DB2 table. A stack is a table that is equipped to do first-in, last-out processing, as has been discussed in the chapter on data structures. To accomplish this type of processing requires the use of a variable, often called the *pointer* or *stack pointer*. The dynamics of a stack are described in the chapter on data relationships and structures in DB2.

Each entry into the stack contains two pieces of information: the part that is the subassembly—STACK.CURR—for the level previously accessed, and the associated level count—STACK.SUB. For example, for the simple bill of material that has been discussed, if part 1053 is being exploded, then the part 5096 would be put on the stack with the level count of one. (Level count equals one because 5096 is the first subassembly of part 1053.) The stack then contains a map of the path down the bill of material that is being processed at any moment in time.

The algorithm used to process a bill of material explosion is illustrated by

```
EXPLODE = 'Y'
POINTER = 0
ACTIVE = 'xxx. . .'
NEXT = 1
DO WHILE EXPLODE = 'Y'
        SELECT PARTPTR
        FROM TABLE.DOWN
        WHERE PART.DOWN = ACTIVE AND
              NEXT = PART.LEVEL.COUNT
        IF PARTPTR FOUND THEN DO
              OUTPUT ACTIVE
              POINTER = POINTER + 1
              STACK.CURR(POINTER) = ACTIVE
              STACK.SUB(POINTER) = NEXT + 1
              ACTIVE = PARTPTR
              NEXT = 1
              END
        IF PARTPTR NOT FOUND THEN DO
              IF POINTER = 0 THEN EXPLODE = 'N'
              IF POINTER > 0 THEN DO
                    OUTPUT ACTIVE
                    ACTIVE = STACK.CURR(POINTER)
                    NEXT = STACK.SUB(POINTER)
                    POINTER = POINTER - 1
              END
        END
END
```

In the algorithm the part to be exploded is loaded into the field ACTIVE. The control variable NEXT is set to 1. NEXT will control the level count for each new level of explosion that is required. The control variable EXPLODE determines when the explosion has finished, and the control variable POINTER controls which level of the stack is being operated on. The stack contains two fields: CURR and SUB. CURR indicates the part that is being worked on, and SUB contains the level count.

The algorithm retrieves one part after the next, beginning with the part to be exploded. The order of retrieval is based on the logical structure of the bill of material. When a PARTPTR is found, it is exploded and its position is recursively "remembered." After it is exploded, processing continues with the next part at the same level (whose level count is one greater than the part that has been exploded).

Note that the downward table does not have to be indexed. It can be randomly sequenced and unindexed, although for a large bill of material an index on the keys of the downward table will improve performance by not requiring a full table scan each time a part is sought.

IMPLOSIONS

The algorithm has shown the activities for a downward explosion of a bill of materials. An upward explosion is possible using the upward table, although in practice an upward explosion often does not make sense. When an upward explosion is done, it is called an *implosion*. The processing logic required for an implosion is almost identical to the logic required for an explosion.

A RECURSIVE INFINITE LOOP

One of the anomalies of the algorithm for explosion is the possibility of an infinite loop being encountered in the structure of the bill of material. If a part ever appears as its own subassembly, even several levels removed, the bill of material is logically in an infinite loop. There is no technical reason why an infinite loop cannot be created by an unaware production control analyst. As a consequence, the programmer needs to verify that an infinite loop does not exist in the bill of material structure.

Fortunately, checking for an infinite loop by using the explosion algorithm is easy to do. The data stored in the stack of the algorithm represents the active leg of the structure that is under analysis. If any part is repeated in the stack, then there is an infinite loop in the structure. Code can be written to check the contents of the stack every time a new entry is about to be placed on the stack.

```
                    .
                    .
                    .

        CHECKER = POINTER
        LOOP = 'N'
        DO WHILE CHECKER > 0
```

```
                    IF STACK.CURR(CHECKER) = PARTPTR
                    THEN LOOP = 'Y'
                    CHECKER = CHECKER - 1
          END
          IF LOOP = 'Y' THEN . . .
                    .
                    .
                    .
```

The simple subroutine merely verifies that the new PARTPTR encountered is not already on the STACK. If the part is already on the STACK, then the variable LOOP will equal 'Y' and an infinite loop will have been detected. Upon detection, appropriate action can be taken.

OTHER BILL OF MATERIAL PROCESSING

The bill of material processing that has been discussed is made complex by the fact that a level count is required for every part. Building and maintaining the level count field is artificial and awkward, although for some processes it is necessary. There are other design alternatives that may apply in special cases.

When level count is part of the data structure, the bill of material could be large or small; the processing of the algorithm is indifferent to the size of the bill of material. Suppose the bill of material to be exploded is not large or that there is plenty of main memory in which to do stack processing. Then the complexity introduced by the level count in the first explosion process discussed is not necessary. Level count can be discarded, and the explosion can be done somewhat differently.

Suppose the parts data bases are designed as described, except there is no level count field. Then the following algorithm can be used to process the bill of material explosion.

```
EXPLODE = 'Y'
POINTER = 0
ACTIVE = 'xxx. . .'
DO WHILE EXPLODE = 'Y'
        SELECT PARTPTR
        FROM TABLE.DOWN
        WHERE PART.DOWN = ACTIVE
        IF PARTPTR FOUND THEN DO
                OUTPUT ACTIVE
                LOOP = 'Y'
                DO WHILE LOOP = 'Y'
                        POINTER = POINTER + 1
                        FETCH PARTPTR INTO STACK.CURR(POINTER)
                        IF SQLCODE = 100 THEN LOOP = 'N'
        END
```

```
ACTIVE = STACK.CURR(POINTER)
POINTER = POINTER - 1
END
IF PARTPTR NOT FOUND THEN DO
        IF POINTER = 0 THEN EXPLODE = 'N'
        IF POINTER > 0 THEN DO
                OUTPUT ACTIVE
                ACTIVE = STACK.CURR'POINTER)
                POINTER = POINTER - 1
        END
    END
END
```

ALGORITHMIC DIFFERENCES

The first algorithm for bill of material explosion processing that was discussed can be termed a *level count* algorithm in which individual subassemblies were processed one at a time, using the field level count to individually sequence the parts. The second bill of material explosion algorithm that was discussed did not require the level count field and processed subassemblies set at a time.

There are several differences between the previously discussed level count explosion and the set processing explosion. One difference is that sets of data are processed by the set processing algorithm. The set processing algorithm will require a stack substantially larger than the level count algorithm. Although the set processing algorithm requires more storage, it also is simpler and requires a simpler data structure.

OTHER RECURSIVE STRUCTURES

The structure of the bill of material that has been discussed is called the *generalized* bill of material structure. Although the generalized structure is flexible and suits most needs for bill of material processing, it is hardly the only structuring possible. The logical structure of a bill of material can be turned into an identical physical structure. For example, for a three-level bill of material structure, three levels of information may actually be stored in a single row, or a separate table may be constructed for each level. As long as the bill of material structure is very rigid and as long as there are not too many levels, then there may not be too many problems.

In general, however, defining a bill of material structure in other than the generalized form leads to complexities that are not easily solved.

Another way that recursion is often designed is by building it into the key structure of data. For example, a key of ABCD indicates that A is the finished product, B is an assembly of A, C is a subassembly of B, and that D is a raw good. Embedding recursion in a key structure, in all but the most unusual of cases, is a poor practice. Inevitably the structure is inflexible. Furthermore, the embedded key structure is wrapped up in the code of the system, and when changes need to be made the result is massive disruption of code.

DIFFERENCES BETWEEN LEVELS

The question can be legitimately raised, For a generalized recursive structure, isn't it possible to have differences from one level to the next? The single definition of data in a generalized structure does not easily accommodate the unique differences between levels. For example, suppose a generalized bill of material structure has been built for an organizational structure. Each node in the organization structure has its own manager, its own budget, its own overhead, and so forth. The generalized definition applies as easily to the headquarters as to the departments of a division.

Suppose at the headquarters there were some special needs. A manager at the headquarters level is allocated special funds for research and development that are not applicable at other levels of the organization. A special table can be created away from the bill of material for these special needs that apply to only part of the organization.

ONLINE VERSUS BATCH BILL OF MATERIAL PROCESSING

A final issue relating to bill of material processing is what kinds of processing need to be done in batch and what kinds of processing can be done online. The same principles of division of processing apply to bill of material processing as apply elsewhere. Long-running programs are not run in the online environment. Long-running programs are run in batch. The nature of bill of material explosion or implosion processing is such that it is doubtful if those processes would ever be run in the online environment.

Summary

In summary, this chapter has focused on what a bill of material is, how it needs to be structured, and how that structure is manipulated. Two processes have been identified as complex to execute: an explosion and an implosion. One danger of bill of material processing is the existence of an infinite loop. The infinite loop can be uncovered by verification in the stack.

CHAPTER 10
HIGH AVAILABILITY

This chapter discusses the problems associated with achieving a high degree of system availability in DB2. The issues of online availability center around the number of times the online system goes down and the amount of time required to bring the system back online. The two principal activities that occur during data base downtime are data base recovery and data base reorganization. Techniques for minimizing the resources used for reorganization and recovery are discussed here.

IMPORTANCE OF DESIGN

There are two essential facets to the online environment: online performance and online availability. Performance is designed into the transactions and data bases of the system; performance is not tuned into the system after the fact. Availability is likewise designed into the system, primarily into the data bases of the system.

Data base availability is primarily a function of the downtime of the system. Some aspects of availability are beyond the scope of the application designer. Power supply stability, machine failure, and acts of nature are all beyond the scope of control of the data base designer. Fortunately, most system outages are not caused by uncontrollable factors. Most system outages occur at the application or operational level and in fact are very much influenced by the analyst.

RECOVERY AND REORGANIZATION

The two primary reasons for system unavailability are the activities of recovery and reorganization. Recovery occurs when there is a system failure and the data and transactions of the system need to be restored. Recovery is an unscheduled event, unlike data base reorganization, which is scheduled. Whenever recovery or reorganization are occurring, the data base is unavailable for other processing. The strategy for high availability is to minimize the time required for recovery and reorganization.

PHASES OF RECOVERY

There are three phases to the recovery process. The first phase is the discovery of the error. Data base size is seldom a factor in the discovery phase. The second phase is the analysis required to understand why the error occurred and what to do about the error. Data base size is very much a factor in this phase of recovery. Large data bases often require many resources for diagnostic analysis.

The smaller the data bases, the faster diagnostics can be run. In fact, large data base size may prevent iterative analysis from being done after a failure. Massive amounts of data often mask pertinent information that otherwise would be obvious or at least easy to get to. Exaggerating the effect of data base size is the fact that the second phase of recovery analysis is often the lengthiest phase. Anything that can be done to shorten this phase is beneficial.

```
phase1                  phase2                        phase3
/-------/ /----------------------------/ /-----------------------/
error          diagnosis and  formulation     prescriptive measures
detection
```

Figure 10.1   The three phases of recovery.

The third phase of recovery is the prescriptive phase, in which action is taken as a result of the analysis made in the second phase. Depending on the error and the fix, data base size may play a part in this phase. On occasions a fix can be implemented immediately with no significant data manipulation. In this case data base size is not a factor. In other cases where data bases must be manipulated, data base size is a factor.

The three phases of recovery are shown by Figure 10.1.

To minimize the work done in phase 2 or phase 3 of recovery requires that the units of data on which analysis is being done and on which recovery measures are being taken be minimized. Strictly speaking, the size of the physical unit on which analysis and recovery are done is what needs to be minimized.

REORGANIZATION AS AN UNLOAD AND RELOAD PROCESS

Reorganization occurs for a plethora of reasons. The most common reason for reorganization is the internal disorganization of data at the table and/or at the index level. A reorganization of data has the effect of reconciling the logical and the physical order of data. Disorganized data are physically placed so that the system requires unnecessary I/O to access the data. The degree of organization (or disorganization!) is determined by utilities that monitor the physical placement and access of data.

During a reorganization, data are read in their old state, sorted or modified if necessary, and reloaded in their new state. Once reloaded in the new state, the logical and the physical sequences of the data are synchronized, and the system can access the data efficiently. Because of its functional simplicity, a reorganization is sometimes called an *unload/reload program*.

Figure 10.2 shows the mechanics of a reorganization. When a table is reorganized, its indexes are normally reorganized as well.

Internal disorganization (that is, unoptimal physical placement of data) is not

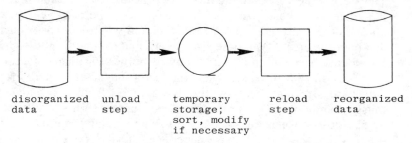

```
disorganized   unload        temporary        reload       reorganized
data           step          storage;         step         data
                             sort, modify
                             if necessary
```

Figure 10.2   The mechanics of data reorganization.

the only reason for reorganization of data. When the structure of data undergoes radical redefinition, the data probably need to be reorganized. The difference between a reorganization for internal cleanliness of data and for radical redefinition of data is important.

Reorganization for internal cleanliness of data may be done for (and may actually affect) relatively few rows of data, but reorganization for structure redefinition is done because of a need to modify every row.

The smaller the data base (down to a point!), the faster the recovery and reorganization. The faster recovery and reorganization can be done, the higher the system availability.

ESTIMATING DOWNTIME

The analyst knows a data base is too large by estimating the time required for recovery and reorganization. To estimate the time needed for the execution of these utilities, the size of the data base must be estimated. Data base size is estimated by calculating the amount of data in the row, the overhead in the row, the number of rows, the free space in the page and the number of free pages, and the space required for an index.

All indexes should be taken into account, and all three levels of index space must be factored in. In addition data base size as the data base goes into full production must be estimated, not just the size of the data base immediately after implementation.

After the size of the data base is estimated, recovery and reorganization time must be calculated. There are several approaches to this calculation. One approach is to compare the recovery needs with a similar table that is already in existence. As long as there are the same number of indexes and as long as row size and the number of occurrences of rows are approximately the same, the comparison is valid, at least in gross terms.

Another approach is to prototype the recovery and reorganization needs. Usually a small amount of data is used in the prototype, and an extrapolation is done. If there is any question as to the recovery and reorganization requirements for a data base, a prototype should be done.

Generally speaking, a prototype is done using either 10 percent of the data that will actually exist or, for large data bases, one spindle's worth of data. In addition, the prototype must include one occurrence of each foreign key relationship that will exist. Another consideration is the representative population of tables, especially tables that are often accessed and have multiple foreign keys.

One factor that cannot be prototyped is the phase 2 recovery time—the time spent in analysis. The time estimations for phase 2 must be added to the estimated or prototyped recovery time, which is really phase 3 time.

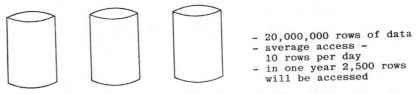

- 20,000,000 rows of data
- average access -
  10 rows per day
- in one year 2,500 rows
  will be accessed

Figure 10.3 In the data bases shown, massive amounts of data will never be accessed.

PROBABILITY OF DOWNTIME

After the estimates for downtime are created, the probability of downtime must be calculated. Generally speaking, the downtime pattern of a shop is constant; some shops experience very few outages and other shops experience frequent outages. The frequency of outages is due to several factors including design, implementation, and operations. The track record of a shop should be the guiding factor in the estimation of the frequency of outages. As a result, it does not matter whether the probability of outage is being calculated for a new system or the rewrite or enhancement of an older system.

The probability of an outage should be considered along with the length of the outage to determine if system availability goals will be met. It is assumed that availability goals have been established formally and in a quantified manner. If system availability goals have not been established, then there can be no objective measurement against the goals.

REDUCING THE VOLUME OF DATA

The following analysis should be done for every large data base that requires a significant amount of uptime.

To reduce the volume of data, the first (very basic) question to be asked is whether all the data is necessary and whether the data will be used. Figure 10.3 shows a data base in which only a small portion of the data base will ever be accessed.

In Figure 10.3, only a portion of the data will ever be accessed. The data that will not be accessed still are expensive to maintain in an automated form.

Analysis should be done to determine what data can be culled from the data base. Typical criteria for culling data include the age of the data, the size of the account that is being represented, the size of the customer whose data is kept, and active data versus inactive data. There are probably infinite numbers of criteria for the culling of data. Each of the criteria serves to separate the data with a high probability of access from the data with a low probability of access.

If there are large volumes of data that will never or very infrequently be accessed, then clearly some reduction of data is in order.

On occasion the system requirements will specify that data is needed but that only very infrequently will some of the data be accessed. At this point the economics of user requirements enter the picture. What is the cost of storing and maintaining data online when it will seldom be needed?

Most likely a more cost-effective alternative is to store the data offline on magnetic tape or other media. Offline storage does not mean that the data cannot be accessed, but that access to the data will be slower than online access. The costs of offline storage and offline access are much lower than the corresponding online costs. The utility of fast access and slower access must be measured against the associated costs.

The first level of availability analysis questions whether the data is cost justified in the first place. The second level of analysis follows directly from the first. Has there been a conscious and deliberate split of primitive and derived data? (For an in-depth discussion of primitive and derived data, refer to my *Information Engineering for the Practitioner.*)

Generally speaking, primitive data is stored online and derived data is moved offline or closer to the end-user community. One criterion to determine whether data is primitive or derived is that primitive data is vulnerable to update and derived data is not. This criterion fits very nicely with the movement of derived data to offline storage and processing.

The third level of analysis calls for the split of administrative and operational data. The split of the data does not reduce data base size. Instead, it ensures that data is as untangled as possible. Operational data is that data that is directly concerned with the day-to-day operations of the enterprise. Administrative data is that that is related to the administration of the enterprise. For example, in a banking environment, customer and account data are operational. By the same token, employee payroll, insurance processing, and salary administration data are administrative.

The splitting of administrative and operational data does not imply that neither one should be online (as was the implication of the split of primitive and derived data). Instead, the separation of administrative and operational data allows the data and the accompanying processes to be moved to separate systems if need be, or enables one set of data to recover or reorganize independent of the other. A failure in the operational world will have no effect on the administrative world and vice versa.

The fourth level of analysis calls for the separation and segregation of one application from the next. Unlike the split between administrative and operational data, the split of applications into their own distinct units is not easily accomplished after the system has been designed. If this split is to be done, it is most effective to split the data prior to the building of actual data bases.

However, like the split of operational and administrative data, no data is purged from the online environment. Data is separated into small units so that recovery and reorganization can be done quickly and independently on each unit. The failure of one unit has no effect on other units, further enhancing the availability posture.

The fifth level of analysis occurs for single applications that are large and still have an availability exposure. For a single application, consideration must be given to the splitting of the application according to the key values of the data

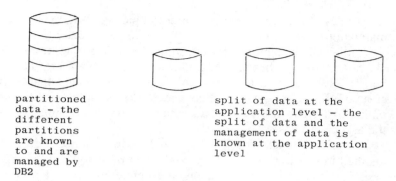

partitioned
data – the
different
partitions
are known
to and are
managed by
DB2

split of data at the
application level – the
split of data and the
management of data is
known at the application
level

Figure 10.4   The two ways an application's data can be split and managed in DB2.

bases. The total amount of data is not reduced; instead, the data is spread over distinct units, each of which is smaller than the collective data base.

There are two ways to reduce the unit of recoverability in DB2 when data is split within the application. One way is by the partitioning of data at the system level. DB2 allows a data base to be partitioned in up to sixty-four partitions. Each partition has the same physical definition, that is, the same physical data base design. The difference between one partition and the next is the content of data.

In DB2 data is partitioned on one and only one key. A partition can be recovered or reorganized independently in most cases. There are two drawbacks to the partitioning of data. One drawback is that if a reorganization is being done to restructure data, all partitions must be reorganized. In this case partitioning does not reduce the unit of recovery. The second case in which partitioning will not enhance availability is the case in which one or more partitions need to be transferred to another processor and/or another copy of DB2. In this case, partitioning of data is not an advantage.

Another technique for the splitting of data across units of recovery is in the physical definition of multiple data bases. One data base contains all keys whose first digit is 0, another data base contains all keys whose first digit is 1, and so forth. This technique is sometimes called placing data in *like* data bases or in *like* partitions. Figure 10.4 illustrates the two options for the splitting of data.

For partitions that are managed at the system level, there is no difference among the definitions of the different like partitions. The only difference from one partition to the next is in the content of the data. One disadvantage of specifying like partitions of data is in the number of control blocks generated. If there are many like partitions, then many control blocks will be generated.

The second disadvantage of building like partitions is that the system is totally unaware of the relationship between any two partitions. In the case of system-managed partitions, the system was aware of the relationship between any two partitions. In the eventuality that *all* the like partitions need to be recovered or reorganized, the system is not aware of any need for coordination.

A major advantage of like partitions of data is that each like data base can be reorganized and recovered independently. The unit of reorganization and recov-

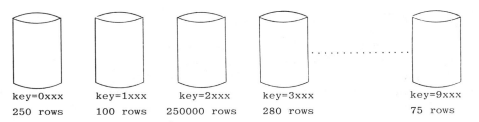

Figure 10.5 Even though the keys appear to be evenly split, the distribution of data does not follow in an even manner.

ery has been reduced to a minimum for all cases. Another advantage of like partitions is that one partition can be moved to another processor and/or copy of DB2 with no concern for the effect on other like partitions. Unlike system-partitioned data that need to be controlled in their entirety, like data can be managed independently. Not only does the ability to move data across processors enhance availability, but it can enhance performance as well.

Splitting data across an application has many ramifications, each of which must be considered by the analyst. One consideration is the interface with other applications. If one application has a key split by line of business and another application has a key split by marketing division, then interfacing the two systems may be complex. Furthermore, splitting both of them onto separate processors may prove difficult if there is any amount of interaction between the systems at all.

A second consideration of splitting data is in the effectiveness of the split. If a data base is split into ten like partitions, but 90 percent of the data resides in a single partition, then the split has not been effective. Figure 10.5 shows such an occurrence.

Moreover, the analyst must consider not just today's data and distribution of data but must factor in tomorrow's trends.

One of the significant advantages of splitting data—at the system or the application level—is that the impact of failure is limited. Not only does recovery occur more quickly, but also fewer data are impacted by the failure. Consider a large data base that is not split. Suppose the data base experiences a failure. Because of its size, recovery takes a long time and much data are made unavailable as the recovery is effected.

REFERENTIAL INTEGRITY AND HIGH AVAILABILITY

One of the advantages of application support of referential integrity is that no data relationships are supported by direct pointers. A data relationship supported by referential integrity goes through an index as one table points to another. There are no hard-coded addresses between one table and the other. The implication is that one table can be recovered independently of another table, which reduces the time required for reorganization.

Summary

In summary, this chapter has discussed the issues of availability from the perspective of the options that are available to the designer. The reduction of the raw amount of data was the first step the designer could take. Next the designer could separate derived data from primitive data. Next the separation of administrative and operational data, as well as the separation of data by application, was considered. Finally, the splitting of data bases within the same application was shown to allow the designer reduction of the data into as fine a unit of recovery and reorganization as desired.

CHAPTER 11
ARCHIVAL PROCESSING AND DB2

Archival processing of data is that processing that is done on aged data, usually looking for one or two records of data or looking at a large amount of data to determine trends that have occurred over time. In almost every case, archival processing is done irregularly. Archival processing is seldom scheduled and usually done heuristically and iteratively (sharing many common characteristics with classical decision support processing).

Strictly speaking, archival processing is not done in a production data processing environment in most companies. (Of course, in a few organizations, archival processing forms the backbone of the work of the company.) Even when archival processing is not done in the mainstream production processing, archival processing usually enhances and complements production processing. Separating work and data into the archival environment frees resources for higher priority production processing.

CRITERIA FOR SUCCESS

The criteria for success in the archival environment are very different from the criteria for success in other environments. High performance, high availability over long periods of time, and rapid system development are normally not high-priority criteria in the archival environment, as they are in other environments. Only the management of large amounts of data is a common criterion of success that is shared by the archival environments and the typical production environment.

In the archival environment, there are usually massive amounts of data, even larger volumes of data than those found in the largest production environment. The management of very large amounts of data is perhaps the single most important criterion of success in the archival environment.

The nature of archival processing is the storage of data for future, unknown needs. Traditionally, analysis of archival data has been done in a heuristic manner. There are essentially two types of archival processing: processing to find a few records out of many and processing massive amounts of data. For example, the archival analyst may search a company's files and records to locate all sales made in New Mexico where state tax has been calculated at 3.5 percent between the first of May 1962 and the sixth of July 1962. Only a few records would satisfy these criteria, and the search would resemble looking for the needle in a haystack.

The other type of archival analysis done is the search and manipulation of massive amounts of data. For example, the archival analyst might wish to determine the average length of time between purchases for those customers making multiple purchases between 1981 and 1985. The satisfaction of this analysis requires much manipulation of data.

ARCHIVAL MEDIA

The media on which archival data are stored have a profound influence on the archival analysis that can be done. The primary division of archival storage media is between two categories: electronic reproducible or nonelectronic reproducible media. Examples of an electronic reproducible medium are magnetic tape and standard DASD.

An example of nonelectronic reproducible media is microfiche. Once data are put off onto microfiche, searches for single records can be done fairly efficiently if the key of the record desired is known, but massive access and manipulation of data are expensive and awkward in microfiche. Data on nonelectronic reproducible media is inexpensive to store and relatively secure from damage.

When data is placed on an electronic reproducible medium, massive manipulation of the data can be done (as well as searches for single records). The cost of storage on electronic reproducible media is relatively expensive, and on occasion whole volumes of data become damaged and are not easily replaced or restored.

Based upon the type of archival analysis that needs to be done, the appropriate medium must be selected. If massive manipulation of archival data is to be done, then an electronic reproducible medium should be selected.

Far and above all other issues, the management of massive volumes of data is the overriding issue of archival processing. Much archival data exist, and at the rate at which archival data typically grow, the volume of data mounts rapidly.

PRIMITIVE ARCHIVAL DATA

The most effective storage of archival data is at the primitive level. Because archival data is stored for unknown usage, the most basic, most detailed data needs to be stored. If a unit of data is not stored for future archival needs, then it is permanently lost (that is, when any primitive unit of data in the production environment is deleted from the production environment and not archived, it is permanently lost). Derived data can be stored in the archival environment as well. Once detailed, primitive data are archived, and the data form the basis for reconciliation of DSS processing and other archival analysis at a later point in time.

Archival data should be stored with a definition that is as "universal" as possible. In other words, the physical layout (that is, the definition) of archival data should be stored in a manner that will facilitate future retrieval. A simple character definition of a field may waste some space, but will simplify the job of future analysts who are trying to use the data. In addition, the physical format should be in as popular and widely used a form as possible. It is a good bet that a simple VSAM layout will present less of a barrier to future usage than will a format from some less popular software or access method.

In addition to the content of data being archived, the format of data should be archived as well. The format should contain the field name, the data characteristics, and any pertinent information about the field that will help future archival analysts understand the meaning and content of the archival data that are available. In addition, any tables that are referenced or any encoding or decoding of archived data that has been done should likewise be referenced and stored.

In general, data relationships in archival files are kept to a minimum if they are kept at all.

SUBJECT ORIENTATION

The orientation of archival data is toward the major subjects of the organization, as are the standard operational data bases derived from the business of the enterprise. For example, customer information should be stored with other related customer information. In the same vein, activity information should be stored with other activity information. Separating and storing archival data according to the major subjects of the enterprise prepare the information for future usage in that there is not a confused intermingling of different types of data.

Over time, detailed, process-oriented aspects of the major subjects of the enterprise are sure to change, but the major subjects of the enterprise—customers, activities, accounts, the enterprise—are slow to change. The orientation of the archival data bases to the major subjects of the organization (which is the same orientation as the operational data bases) provides a straightforward basis for the flow of data from the operational to the archival environment.

The applicability of DB2 to archival data is at first glance severely limited. The volume of data, the infrequency of access, and the inability to predict the usage of the data all present special problems to the DB2 archival analyst. For example, the sheer volume of archival data normally precludes the indexing of *any* of the data, a severe limitation to the usefulness of the DB2 software. Another problem is that the masses of data stored before DB2 became widely available may not be able to be conveniently translated into a format known to DB2. Even if a conversion from an existing format to a DB2 format can be done, the overhead entailed is potentially very large. As a consequence, DB2 is not applicable to the standard archival environment.

THE LIVING SAMPLE ENVIRONMENT

There is one archival environment to which DB2 is peculiarly applicable. It is called the *living sample* environment, and DB2 is truly an ideal tool for that environment.

The living sample environment is best described in terms of some examples. Suppose an archival analyst were to analyze ten years of historical data. The analyst determines that the average sale over the ten-year period was $105.36, that the busiest day of the year was December 16, and that 87 percent of sales were conducted with credit cards. To arrive at those conclusions, the archival analyst went through 750,000 individual transactions that occurred from 1976 to 1986.

Now suppose another analyst is operating from a living sample archival data base. A living sample data base is made up of representative samples of data and is periodically refreshed (thus the term *living sample*). There are 10,000 representative transactions in the living sample data base. The archival analyst operating against the living sample data base determines that the average sale is $104.96, that the busiest day of the year is December 17, and that 85.6 percent of business is conducted through credit cards.

There is no doubt that the first archival analyst has a more accurate answer than the living sample analyst. There is likewise no doubt that the cost of processing actual archival data is *very* expensive. The worth of the accuracy of the analysis of the archival data is questionable. The living sample archival analyst has arrived at very close to the same conclusion as the archival analyst, but the living sample analyst has processed 1/75 as many records. Unless there is an unusual need for a high degree of accuracy, the second analyst using living sample data has arrived at satisfactory conclusions much more efficiently than the analyst using classical archival data.

DB2 is an ideal tool for the living sample environment. There is not so much data in the living sample environment that the environment cannot be managed by DB2. Indexes can be created as data is periodically refreshed. The living sample DSS analyst in DB2 has the full gamut of DB2 options with which to analyze data.

Furthermore, many of the constraints of the production environment, such as using designed transactions, are not necessary in the living sample environment.

TIME STAMPING DATA

Practically all of the data in the living sample environment will be *time stamped*. A time stamp is merely an appendage of the key indicating the value or status of a key as of some moment in time. For example, an account may be archived periodically. In September 1986, account 3650 contained $1584.00. The domicile of the account is the Market Street branch, and the date the account was opened was May 1979. The key of the record would be account, year, and month. On the first of October a "snapshot" of the September data is taken and archived.

There are two ways that archived data is time stamped: with a discrete time value and with a continuous time value. A discrete time value represents the values of data elements as of a single point in time. As an example of discrete data, the balance in account 3650 as of 10 A.M. was $500 when the owner of the account wrote a check for $250. Each of the pieces of data about the transaction is an example of discrete data.

A continuous time value has a beginning and an ending time value and represents data as having the values contained for the entire length of time measured by the continuous dates. For example, the bank pays 5.5% interest on passbook accounts from January 1985 to July 1987. A continuous time stamp record would contain a key—the type of account, the beginning date the rate was paid, the ending date the rate was paid—and the rate itself.

Continuous time stamping is most appropriate to small numbers of data elements that change infrequently. Every time a variable changes values, a new continuous record must be created. The history of the passbook rate is an example of continuous time stamp data.

Continuous data normally maintains a simple continuity—where the ending date of the earlier record is one unit of time less than the beginning date of the later continuous record. However, simple continuity is not the only choice. On occasion, discontinuous or overlapping records may need to be kept.

```
ACCT                    char(10)    /*key*/
ACCT.DATE
ACCT.DATE.MONTH         pic'99'     /*key*/
ACCT.DATE.DAY           pic'99'     /*key*/
ACCT.TYPE               char(1)
ACCT.BALANCE            dec fixed(9,2)
```

Figure 11.1 Data layout for the account balance table.

Another consideration is the beginning date of the first continuous time span record and the ending date of the last continuous time span record. These dates may have an actual value, or these dates may be open-ended. For example, if the ending datum for the last continuous time span record equals infinity, then the time span information is valid indefinitely, until further update can occur. But if the ending date has a value, then the set of continuous records has a finite ending.

Discrete snapshot data is applicable to large amounts of data that rapidly change (as opposed to continuous time span data). A major concern of discrete time variant data is the frequency of snapshots. Snapshots taken too frequently will be voluminous and may actually mask long-term trends. Snapshots taken not frequently enough will lose important fluctuations of data.

An issue applicable to both discrete and continuously measured data is that of the unit of measurement. For example, a measurement of a checking account balance by year does not make sense, and the measurement of the Dow-Jones Industrial Average by the minute does not make sense. The unit of time used to measure time variant data must be appropriate to the data.

One of the disciplines of the creation of the living sample environment is in the preservation of the complete data needs of the environment. Very often archival data is made up of the "refuse" of the operational environment. Only those data elements that are being purged from the operational environment are sent to the archival environment.

While newly purged data may well belong in the archival environment, other data that may not be purged ought to be in the archival environment in order to present a clear picture for archival processing. Establishing and using the living sample environment bring to light the complete set of needs of the archival analyst. Another advantage of DB2 in the living sample environment is the orientation of DB2 towards set processing. The time stamping that occurs arranges data conveniently into sets.

As an example of how DB2 tables might be processed as time variant tables, consider the following examples.

Two tables are defined to DB2 containing archival data. The account table contains account identification, the balance of the account as of the fifteenth of the month, and an identification of the type of loan associated with the account. Figure 11.1 shows the layout of the data for the account table.

The table in Figure 11.1 is recognized as discrete time variant data. The loan table contains continuous time variant data. The loan table contains a key of loan type and the beginning date and ending date of the loan, as well as the effective rate during the time span. The loan rows are arranged so that they continuously define all the days of the year. In other words, the beginning date of row $n + 1$ is

```
LOAN.TYPE                     char(1)        /*key*/
LOAN.BEG.DATE
LOAN.BEG.DATE.MONTH           pic'99'        /*key*/
LOAN.BEG.DATE.DAY            pic'99'        /*key*/
LOAN.END.DATE
LOAN.END.DATE.MONTH           pic'99'        /*key*/
LOAN.END.DATE.DAY            pic'99'        /*key*/
LOAN.RATE                     dec fixed(5,4)      Figure 11.2
```

one day less than the ending date of row *n*. Figure 11.2 shows the table layout for the loan table.

There are several other variables that are needed. Cumulative rate is simply the variable used to store values that will be calculated. The variable CALC. DATE is used to control the iterations of the algorithm. Figure 11.3 shows the definitions of the variables.

```
CALC.DATE
CALC.MONTH           pic'99'
CALC.DAY             pic'99'

CUMRATE              dec fixed(11,3)    Figure 11.3
```

Some sample occurrences of the account and the rate table are shown by Figure 11.4.

The account table and the loan table are relationally defined, but they cannot be joined in the normal sense. Even though the date fields enjoy a logical intersection of data, the actual physical join is more difficult to implement.

Consider a simple logical join. Suppose the interest paid for an account for a year is to be calculated. The balance in one table is to be multiplied by the applicable rate in the other table.

The algorithm shown in Figure 11.5 merges the two tables based on the intersection of dates.

Twelve calculations are made for an account for a year. The rate that is applicable as of the fifteenth of the month is multiplied by the balance and is divided by 12 (there are twelve accumulations made per year).

The value accumulated in CUMRATE roughly approximates the interest paid by an account for a year.

A finer calculation may be required. The simple calculation made for each month assumes that the interest rate is constant from the fifteenth of the month

```
ACCT=0056          ACCT=0056          ACCT=0056          ......
date=Jan15         date=Feb15         date=Mar15         ......
balance=100051.32  balance=99997.61   balance=99926.31   ......


RATE='L'           RATE='L'           RATE='L'           .......
begdate=Jan1       begdate=Jan6       begdate=Jan16      .......
enddate=Jan5       enddate=Jan15      enddate=Feb3       .......
rate=.053          rate=.057          rate=.059          .......
```

Figure 11.4 Sample occurrences of the account and rate tables.

```
CUMRATE=0
CALC.MONTH=1
CALC.DAY=15
DO WHILE CALC.MONTH < 13
    SELECT ACCT.BALANCE ACCT.TYPE
    FROM ACCT.TABLE
    WHERE ACCT='xxx...' AND ACCT.DATE=CALC.DATE
    SELECT LOAN.RATE
    FROM RATE.TABLE
    WHERE LOAN.TYPE=ACCT.TYPE AND
        LOAN.BEG.DATE =< CALC.DATE AND LOAN.END.DATE >= CALC.DATE
    CUMRATE=CUMRATE+((LOAN.RATExACCT.BALANCE)/12)
    CALC.MONTH=CALC.MONTH+1
    END
```

Figure 11.5

being calculated to the fifteenth of the next month, but such is not the case. The rate is variable and may change many times throughout the month.

A finer, more precise calculation, done on a day-by-day basis, is shown by Figure 11.6.

In Figure 11.6, each day's interest is calculated. If rates change, then a new SQL call is made to retrieve the new daily rate.

The example shows how two time variant files can be "joined" logically even though a physical join is not possible. The balance file is time stamped with

```
CUMRATE=0
CALC.MONTH=1
CALC.DAY=15
DO WHILE CALC.MONTH < 13
    SELECT ACCT.BALANCE ACCT.TYPE
    FROM ACCT.TABLE
    WHERE ACCT='xxx...' AND ACCT.DATE=CALC.DATE
    SELECT LOAN.RATE
    FROM RATE.TABLE
    WHERE ACCT.TYPE=LOAN.TYPE AND
        LOAN.BEG.DATE =< CALC.DATE AND LOAN.END.DATE >= CALC.DATE
    DAYPROC='N'
    DO WHILE DAYPROC='N'
        CUMRATE=CUMRATE+((ACCT.BALANCExLOAN.RATE)/365)
        CALC.DAY=CALC.DAY+1
        IF CALC.DAY=32 AND IF CALC.MONTH=2 THEN DO
            CALC.MONTH=2
            CALC.DAY=1
            END
        IF CALC.DAY=29 THEN IF CALC.MONTH=2 THEN DO
            CALC.MONTH=3
            CALC.DAY=1
            END
            :   :   :   :   :   :   :   :   :
            :   :   :   :   :   :   :   :   :
        IF CALC.DAY > LOAN.END.DATE THEN DO
            SELECT LOAN.RATE
            FROM RATE.TABLE
            WHERE LOAN.TYPE=ACCT.TYPE AND
                LOAN.BEG.DATE =< CALC.DATE AND LOAN.END.DATE >= CALC.DATE
            END
        IF CALC.DAY=15 THEN DAYCALC='Y'
    END
```

Figure 11.6

discrete data, the rate file is time stamped with continuous data, and they are logically merged based on matching key values and logically intersecting data values.

However, logical joins are not the only challenge facing the archival analyst.

EFFICIENT ACCESS OF ARCHIVAL DATA

Some problems are endemic to the archival environment. Although the problems will be illustrated within the context of DB2 processing, it is noted that *any* data management software would experience the same problems.

One problem facing the archival analyst is the arrangement of data so that efficient access can be made. This is the same problem facing the analyst in other circumstances, except that in the case of archival data the massive amounts of data and the way the data are collected and accessed present some peculiar problems.

As an example, suppose each month on the fifteenth of the month account balance information is stripped from production files. The bulk of the data will be loaded into an archival file. If the data are unclustered in the archival file (which is extremely likely, because there are normally so much data that no indexes can be built), the data will be loaded in a sequential fashion. Assuming that the data are loaded sequentially (that is, loaded in the same sequence as collected), Figure 11.7 shows how a physical page might look after being loaded from the January strip.

There is nothing inherently wrong with the approach of simply loading data from an archival file as stripped and time stamped. However, consider the result of this process as it places data over several pages, as shown by Figure 11.8.

Consider the work done by the system to analyze the balance of a given account over several months or years. The system must go to a new page for every month's activity. Twelve I/Os will be needed to access twelve months' data for an account, even if DB2 knows in which pages the data reside.

If it appears that single account analysis will be a normal archival analytical activity (that is, an analytical activity that occurs on a fairly frequent basis), then a different organization of data is required.

The data need to be clustered on an index based on account data, but merely clustering the data (assuming that the data *can* be clustered!) may not be adequate. Unless *much* free space is left in the page when the first entry is inserted, the clustering of data can lead to horrendous data management problems as later inserts are made.

In addition to the clustering of data, the data can be loaded in the following manner. On the January load (assuming the archival data bases are created in January), the data for the month of January is entered. At the same time, dummy

ACCOUNT	001	002	003	...
DATE	Jan15	Feb15	Mar15	...
balance	nnn	nnn	nnn	...

Figure 11.7 Sequential unclustered loading of data.

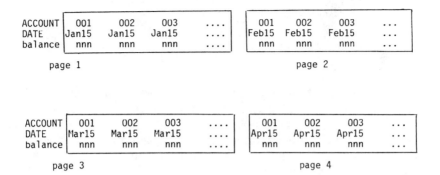

ACCOUNT	001	002	003	....
DATE	Jan15	Jan15	Jan15	....
balance	nnn	nnn	nnn	....

page 1

	001	002	003	...
	Feb15	Feb15	Feb15	...
	nnn	nnn	nnn	...

page 2

ACCOUNT	001	002	003	....
DATE	Mar15	Mar15	Mar15	....
balance	nnn	nnn	nnn	....

page 3

	001	002	003	...
	Apr15	Apr15	Apr15	...
	nnn	nnn	nnn	...

page 4

Figure 11.8

entries are inserted for February, March, and so forth. The dummy entries contain key values and null values for nonkey data. Figure 11.9 shows a few pages after the January load.

In February (and in subsequent months) data are replaced, not inserted. With the resulting organization of data, a single account's activity can be accessed in one I/O, not twelve.

Storage and management of data that occurs or is measured at predictable intervals are relatively simple. Data that occurs or is measured randomly present entirely different challenges to the archival analyst and designer.

For example, suppose an archival analyst wishes to store information about the checks written by banking customers. Some customers write many more checks than other customers, and the number of checks written one month may vary significantly from another month for a single customer.

One approach is simply to store, by month, all the checks written by all customers. All the checks written are gathered into a monthly file. The gathering of the information is easy and natural, but the utilization of the files can present fearsome problems. To retrieve information, the first qualification must be on date (or at least month). For some types of processing, this division of data may not be

ACCOUNT	001	001	001	....
DATE	Jan15	Feb15	Mar15	....
balance	nnn	nnn	nnn	....

page 1

	002	002	002	...
	Jan15	Feb15	Mar15	...
	nnn	nnn	nnn	...

page 2

ACCOUNT	003	003	003	....
DATE	Jan15	Feb15	Mar15	....
balance	nnn	nnn	nnn	....

page 3

	004	004	004	...
	Jan15	Feb15	Mar15	...
	nnn	nnn	nnn	...

page 4

Figure 11.9

```
rate type='L'        rate type='L'        rate type='L'           .....
dates=Jan1-Jan6      dates=Jan7-Feb14     dates=Feb15-Feb28       .....
rate=.053            rate=.058            rate=.061               .....
limit=1000           limit=1000           limit=1000              .....
```

Figure 11.10

much of a problem. However, consider the work the analyst must do in tracking the customers' running balances from one month to the next.

A second option is to reserve as much space as is normally needed for a customer for a year. Each month the checking activities are loaded into the space reserved for them by individual customer account. However, there are some problems with this approach. Suppose thirty-five "slots" are allocated each month for each customer's checking activity. One month a customer has used only fifteen slots. What happens to the unused slots? Another month a customer uses (or needs) sixty slots. Where do the extra slots come from?

These questions can certainly be answered, but the complexity and management challenges can be severe.

INTEGRITY AND ACCURACY OF ARCHIVAL DATA

Another typical problem facing the designer is that of maintaining the integrity and accuracy of data. For example, consider the problems of the programmer in the maintenance of continuous time span data. Updates or creations of data can cause very complex problems when one or more rows of data participate in a continuous definition of a time span. Figure 11.10 shows some continuous time span rows. In the data shown in Figure 11.10, rate type = 'L', loan limit = 1000, and the rate varies from day to day. Each of the rows begins one unit beyond where the previous row ends. In other words, the first row's logical end is on January 6. The next beginning date must be January 7; otherwise, there would be a discontinuity of the data. Note too that there is no overlap of data defined by two or more rows; that is, for any given point in time defined by the continuous time span, there is one and only one set of values that are applicable.

Now suppose the following transaction were entered: Change the limit value of loans to 1,500 for the dates of January 4 to January 20. In this case transaction variables are TX.BEG = Jan 4, TX.END = Jan 20, and TX.LIMIT = 1500. TX.RATE = 0 (or null values), indicating that rate is not affected by the transaction.

The data after the update has been applied to the continuous time span shown in Figure 11.10 is shown in Figure 11.11. Several new rows have been

```
rate type='L'    rate type='L'    rate type='L'     rate type='L'      rate type='L'      ...
dates=Jan1-Jan3  dates=Jan4-Jan6  dates=Jan7-Jan20  dates=Jan21-Feb14  dates=Feb15-Feb28  ...
rate=.053        rate=.053        rate=.058         rate=.058          rate=.061          ...
limit=1000       limit=1500       limit=1500        limit=1000         limit=1000         ...
```

Figure 11.11

```
TX.BEG        dec fixed (5,0)    /*key*/
TX.END        dec fixed (5,0)
TX.RATE       dec fixed (5,0)
TX.LIMIT      dec fixed (11,2)              Figure 11.12
```

created, and some existing rows have been updated. The continuity of the data remains the same.

The data were updated by means of the following algorithm: Suppose the transaction has a beginning and ending date of TX.BEG and TX.END. If a nonkey field is to be updated—in this case LIMIT and RATE—the field to be updated has a value greater than zero. If a nonkey field is not to be updated, it has a null value. Suppose the DB2 table has (for the data portion of the key) the field DB.BEG. For the purposes of the algorithm to be discussed assume that the RATE.TYPE of the key has been satisfied (in other words, assume that only the continuous dates must be matched between the transaction and the data base.)

The continuous time span data base is indexed and clustered, with a data layout shown by Figure 11.12. Note that the key of the data base is the beginning date, not the beginning and ending date. Ending date is not needed for uniqueness.

The algorithm needed to service the continuous time span data structure is shown in ALGO. (Because of its size, ALGO is shown on pages 158 to 161 at the end of the chapter.)

FOREIGN KEYS IN THE ARCHIVAL ENVIRONMENT

Foreign key relationships are complicated by the volume of data over which the keys interrelate data and the appendage of data onto the key structure of otherwise normal, straightforward relationships. The volume of data and the infrequency of access under normal circumstances

- preclude the use of an index
- preclude the use of a cross-reference table

The remaining choice for relating tables together—dynamically creating the relationship by scanning volumes of data—is likewise unpopular in the face of very large volumes of data. Furthermore, the appendage of data with time stamps—either discrete or continuous—on each key creates logical intersections of data that cannot be joined in the normal manner.

Clearly, special design techniques are required to manage foreign keys in the face of the DB2 archival environment. Some design techniques that can be used separately or in tandem with each other are

- sectioning DB2 data into smaller data bases so that standard foreign key relationships can be implemented
- creating "selective" cross-reference tables, joining selected parts or subsets of tables, not all rows. The selectivity criteria may be on high-dollar items, selected special or trouble accounts, and so on.
- creating time-dependent cross-reference tables (as opposed to general

purpose cross-references). For example, for the year 1986 one cross-reference can be created. Another cross-reference can be created for 1987, and so forth.

- creating selective intersection copies of data that require no further joins. Instead of creating cross-references, data is duplicated and actual intersection tables are created. It must be kept in mind that when data are duplicated (especially archived data) the data must conform to the architectural rules for the management of atomic data.

Summary

DB2 is applicable to the archival environment when living sample processing of archival data is done. In other cases the volume of data prevents the usage of many DB2 features, such as indexing.

Archival data is normally time stamped. Time variant data that is time stamped require special handling. For example, the standard joins of DB2 cannot be done with time-stamped data in the normal manner. Special algorithms are required to actuate the join logically.

Time-stamped data is either continuous or discrete. The volatility of the data, the number of data elements, the usage of the data, and other variables contribute to the decision of how to manage time-variant data.

Continuous Timespan Update Algorithm

```
START:   SELECT DB.BEG  DB.END   DB.BALANCE  B.LIMIT
         FROM RATE.TABLE
         WHERE DB.BEG <=: TX.BEG AND DB.END > =: TX.BEG

         IF TX.BEG < DB.BEG AND IF TX.END < DB.END THEN DO
             NEWRATE = TX.RATE
             NEWLIMIT = TX.LIMIT
             INSERT INTO RATE.TABLE
             VALUES (TX.BEG, DB.BEG-1, NEWRATE, NEWLIMIT)
             ROWBEG = DB.BEG
             NEWRATE = DB.RATE
             IF TX.RATE > O THEN NEWRATE = TX.RATE
             NEWLIMIT = DB.LIMIT
             IF TX.LIMIT >O THEN NEW LIMIT = DB.LIMIT
             UPDATE RATETABLE
             SET  DB.END =: TX.END
                  DB.RATE =: NEWRATE
                  DB.LIMIT =: NEWLIMIT
                  WHERE DB.BEG =: ROWBEG
             INSERT INTO RATE.TABLE
             VALUES (TX.END+1, DB.END, DB.RATE, DB.LIMIT)
             END
```

```
IF TX.BEG < DB.BEG AND IF TX.END = DB.END THEN DO
    NEWRATE = TX.RATE
    NEWLIMIT = TX.LIMIT
    INSERT INTO RATE.TABLE
    VALUES (TX.BEG, DB.BEG-1, NEWRATE, NEWLIMIT)
    ROWBEG = DB.BEG
    NEWRATE = DB.RATE
    IF TX.RATE > 0 THEN NEWRATE = TX.RATE
    NEWLIMIT = DB.LIMIT
    IF TX.LIMIT > 0 THEN NEWRATE = TX.RATE
    UPDATE RATE.TABLE
    SET  DB.END =: TX.END
         DB.RATE =: NEWRATE
         DB.LIMIT =: NEWLIMIT
         WHERE DB.BEG =: ROWBEG
    END
IF TX.BEG < DB.BEG AND IF TX.END > DB.END THEN DO
    NEWRATE = TX.RATE
    NEWLIMIT = TX.LIMIT
    INSERT INTO RATE.TABLE
    VALUES (TX.BEG, DB.BEG-1, NEWRATE, NEW.LIMIT)
    ROWBEG = DB.BEG
    NEWRATE = DB.RATE
    NEWLIMIT = DB.LIMIT
    IF TX.RATE > 0 THEN NEWRATE = TX.RATE
    IF TX.LIMIT > 0 THEN NEWLIMIT = TX.LIMIT
    UPDATE RATE.TABLE
    SET  DB.RATE =: NEWRATE
         DB.LIMIT =: NEWLIMIT
         WHERE DB.BEG =: ROWBEG
    TX.BEG = DB.END+1
    GO TO START
    END
IF TX.BEG = DB.BEG AND IF TX.END < DB.END
    NEWRATE = DB.RATE
    NEWLIMIT = DB.LIMIT
    IF TX.RATE > 0 THEN NEWRATE = TX.RATE
    IF TX.LIMIT > 0 THEN NEWLIMIT = TX.LIMIT
    UPDATE RATE.TABLE
    SET  DB.END =: TX.END
         DB.LIMIT =: NEWLIMIT
         DB.RATE =: NEWRATE
         WHERE DB.BEG =: TX.BEG
    INSERT INTO RATE.TABLE
    VALUES (TX.END+1, DB.END, DB.RATE, DB.LIMIT)
    END
```

```
IF TX.BEG = DB.BEG AND IF TX.END = DB.END THEN DO
     NEWRATE = DB.RATE
     NEWLIMIT = DB.LIMIT
     IF TX.RATE > 0 THEN NEWRATE = TX.RATE
     IF TX.LIMIT > 0 THEN NEWLIMIT = TX.LIMIT
     UPDATE RATE.TABLE
     SET  DB.RATE =: NEWRATE
          DB.LIMIT =: NEWLIMIT
          WHERE DB.BEG =: TX.BEG
     END
IF TX.BEG = DB.BEG AND IF TX.END > DB.END THEN DO;
     NEWRATE = DB.RATE
     NEWLIMIT = DB.LIMIT
     IF TX.RATE >0 THEN NEWRATE = TX.RATE
     IF TX.LIMIT >0 THEN NEWLIMIT = TX.LIMIT
     UPDATE RATE.TABLE
     SET  DB.RATE =: NEWRATE
          DB.LIMIT =: NEWLIMIT
          WHERE DB.BEG =: TX.BEG
     TX.BEG = DB.END+1
     GO TO START
     END
IF TX.BEG > DB.BEG THEN IF TX.END < DB.END THEN DO
     ROWBEG = DB.BEG
     UPDATE RATE.TABLE
     SET DB.END =: TX.BEG-1
     WHERE DB.BEG =: ROWBEG
     NEWRATE = DB.RATE
     NEWLIMIT = DB.LIMIT
     IF TX.RATE >0 THEN NEWRATE = TX.RATE
     IF TX.LIMIT >0 THEN NEWLIMIT = TX.LIMIT
     INSERT INTO RATE.TABLE
     VALUES (TX.BEG, TX.END, NEWRATE, NEWLIMIT)
     INSERT INTO RATE.TABLE
     VALUES (TX.END+1, DB.END, DB.RATE, DB.LIMIT)
     END
IF TX.BEG > DB.BEG THEN IF TX.END = DB.END THEN DO
     ROWBEG = DB.BEG
     UPDATE RATE.TABLE
     SET DB.END =: TX.BEG-1
     WHERE DB.END =: ROWBEG
     NEWRATE = DB.RATE
     NEWLIMIT = DB.LIMIT
     IF TX.RATE > 0 THEN NEWRATE = TX.RATE
     IF TX.LIMIT > 0 THEN NEWLIMIT = TX.LIMIT
     INSERT INTO RATE.TABLE
```

```
                    VALUES (TX.BEG, TX.END, NEWRATE, NEWLIMIT)
                    END
   IF TX.BEG > DB.BEG THEN IF TX.END > DB.END THEN DO
                    ROWBEG = DB.BEG
                    UPDATE RATE.TABLE
                    SET DB.END =: TX.BEG-1
                    WHERE DB.END =: ROWBEG
                    NEWRATE = DB.RATE
                    NEWLIMIT = DB.LIMIT
                    IF TX.RATE > 0 THEN NEWRATE = TX.RATE
                    IF TX.LIMIT > 0 THEN NEWLIMIT = TX.LIMIT
                    INSERT INTO RATE.TABLE
                    VALUES (TX.BEG, DB.END, NEWRATE, NEWLIMIT)
                    TX.BEG = DB.END+1
                    GO TO START
                    END
```

CHAPTER 12

STRATEGIC POSITIONING OF DB2 IN HIGH PERFORMANCE SYSTEMS

DB2 can be used in the high performance environment (such as that found in banking and financial institutions). Institutions that depend on the ability of a DBMS to process large amounts of data and achieve good, consistent response time can use DB2. However, DB2 *must* be used in the right place and in the right way, as further outlined by this chapter. Failure to use DB2 properly will result in inadequate performance that cannot be addressed by tuning or adding larger, more powerful processors.

HIGH PERFORMANCE LEVELS

In banking and in other high performance environments, care must be taken in the strategic usage of DB2 (or of any other piece of software sensitive to online performance and throughput). In the eventuality that a piece of software running on a powerful processor is asked to exceed its throughput capabilities, all of the choices available to the system manager are painful.

A larger processor can be purchased, if one is available that can produce more throughput, but hardware upgrades are expensive and give only a marginal performance boost. Furthermore, if a large, powerful processor is already being used, then no upgrade of processors may be available.

The next option to achieve higher levels of performance is to break the workload onto multiple processors. This is easy to do if DB2 is processing many different types of applications, such as payroll, inventory control, personnel, and bills of materials, but if a single application is being run and is exceeding the capability of the hardware and software, then this option is not applicable.

A third option is to split data running under a single application onto multiple processors. This split can be done only if the applications have been prepared for such a split from the outset. Furthermore, certain applications require the processing of a single data base—not discrete parts of a data base—all at once and cannot allow data to be split across multiple processors. Fortunately, most banking (and other high performance) applications do not fall into this classification.

A final option is to scrap the application and the DBMS and move to a more powerful DBMS. The latter choice always involves significant costs and disruptions. It is never a popular choice. As a consequence, the designer must carefully design the system so that the normal processing capabilities of DB2 are not exceeded or, if the normal processing capabilities of DB2 for a single processor are exceeded, the application can be split over multiple processors into separate workloads.

The normal measurement of software speed running online transactions is in terms of transactions per second. In architecting the high performance environment, careful and constant attention must be paid to the maximum transaction arrival rate that the software will be expected to handle. Once the arrival rate of transactions entering the system begins to exceed the maximum transaction arrival rate, the system reaches the "enqueue" position, where transactions are waiting on other transactions to enter the system.

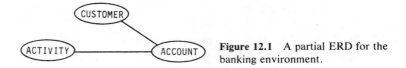

Figure 12.1 A partial ERD for the banking environment.

THE BANKING ENVIRONMENT

The data base designer has completed the conceptual model for the bank and has determined that three subject areas form the backbone of operational processing: account, customer, and activity subject areas, as shown by the ERD in Figure 12.1.

From the high-level subject areas, detailed design follows, and tables are created. The key of an account is 20 bytes, the key of a customer is 15 bytes, and the key of an activity is account number concatenated with date and time, where date (Julian date) and time are fixed bin (31,0) and fixed bin (15,0), respectively. Figure 12.2 shows the physical key structure.

The first two digits of account indicate the region and cycle of an account. A region is a geographic locale. Currently the state being served by the bank is divided into a northern and a southern region (hence, region currently has a maximum value of 2). As the number of customers grows and as the bank prepares to expand beyond the geographical boundaries of a single state, it is anticipated that there may be as many as fifteen regions (in the largest or maximum growth scenario). The second digit of the key indicates the cycle in which an account is placed. Every account is placed into a cycle as the account is opened. There are twenty cycles indicating when a customer's account will have its statement issued. There are currently then forty separate units into which an account may be placed (that is, twenty cycles in two regions).

The twenty cycles correspond to the standard statement cycles of the bank. Every working day (that is, twenty times a month) the bank processes and sends out the statements for a cycle. In such a fashion, the bank avoids a massive month-end effort for the issuing of statements.

The bank currently has two processing centers: the Northern Center and the Southern Center. The accounts (and, in fact, all data) are about equally divided over the two centers. All data is domiciled in one or the other center, but not both (that is, an account is either a Northern or a Southern account). The vast preponderance of data and processing is for activities and accounts. Figure 12.3 shows a typical processing profile for a month, in terms of percentage.

```
Account          -   CHAR (20)
Customer         -   CHAR (15)
Activity/Date/Time - CHAR (20)/Bin Fixed (31,0)/Bin Fixed (15,0)
```

Figure 12.2 Key structures.

```
Activities              58%
Accounts -
   Statementing         20%
   Other                12%
Customer                 8%
Other                    2%
                       ────
                       100%
```
Figure 12.3   Processing profile.

HARDWARE CONFIGURATION

The processing configuration of the hardware is shown by Figure 12.4.

ATM (automated teller machines) and teller processing are organized by region; there are Northern ATM and teller machines and Southern ATM and teller machines. The ATM and teller machines are networked to a centralized processor running IMS Fast Path and IMS Full Function. IMS Fast Path is used for direct teller and ATM processing, and IMS Full Function is used for general purpose processing.

IMS processors in the north and south are interconnected by an MSC (multiple systems coupling) link. The MSC link is used for only a very small percentage of activities. Typically less than 1 percent of processing flows over the MSC link. Only when an account holder who is domiciled in the north attempts to process activity in the south (or vice versa) is the MSC link used. As the activity enters the system, the key of the account is used to determine if the activity should be processed in another center.

As long as there are only two centers for processing, traffic across the MSC is not burdensome. It is anticipated that as the bank expands—especially nationally—traffic over the MSC link will expand.

SYSTEM OF RECORD

Data is organized according to a *system of record* concept. DB2 manages the system of record data, where the actual customer balance is stored nonredundantly. If there is ever any question as to the accuracy of data, reference can be

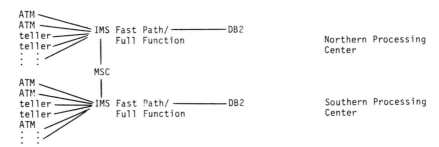

Figure 12.4 The processing configuration of the high-performance banking environment.

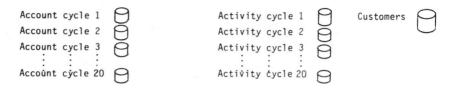

Figure 12.5   Northern DB2 databases.

made to the system of record. When balanced, the system of record contains the accurate value of data, by definition.

In addition to account balance, other data is stored at the DB2 system of record level as well, such as detailed account activity for the last two months and customer data including name, address, age, and credit rating. A sparse amount of data is stored at the Fast Path level. Only the bare information necessary is stored, and it is refreshed nightly from the system of record after balancing. Data found at the Fast Path level typically include account, balance, related accounts, special posting requirements, and any special handling options that might be applicable.

There is no resident data at the ATM level. ATM requests are serviced directly from the Fast Path processor.

The actual data base design at the DB2 level is simple. Tables are connected by foreign keys. The tables are directly derived from the conceptual model. Processing is organized so that any process operates on only a few data bases.

Data base design for Fast Path is likewise simple. All Fast Path data is stored in a single data base segment. Once the I/O is done to retrieve a Fast Path record, the designer is guaranteed that no more I/O need be done. The design and organization of data in the Fast Path environment—not surprisingly—is optimized for performance. In the interest of high performance, data elements that are not necessarily logically related are grouped together.

The denormalization of data in Fast Path for performance overrides the normal data base practices associated with normalization. Note, however, that at the Fast Path level, not many different types of data are affected, and that Fast Path merely holds data in abeyance for rapid access, not data in the system of record.

The IMS processors feed data to DB2, where the system of record resides. DB2 manages the data for accounts, customers, and activities. There are twenty physically separate data bases managed by DB2 for activities and accounts, depending upon what cycle an account for an activity is in, as shown by Figure 12.5.

PEAK-PERIOD PROCESSING RATES

Of special interest are the peak-period processing rates for the different components of the system, as shown by Figure 12.6.

The two rates of interest are rate 1, the ATM to FP rate, and rate 2, the FP

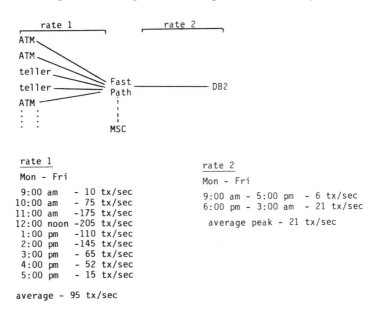

rate 1

Mon - Fri

9:00 am	- 10 tx/sec
10:00 am	- 75 tx/sec
11:00 am	-175 tx/sec
12:00 noon	-205 tx/sec
1:00 pm	-110 tx/sec
2:00 pm	-145 tx/sec
3:00 pm	- 65 tx/sec
4:00 pm	- 52 tx/sec
5:00 pm	- 15 tx/sec

average - 95 tx/sec

rate 2

Mon - Fri

9:00 am - 5:00 pm - 6 tx/sec
6:00 pm - 3:00 am - 21 tx/sec

average peak - 21 tx/sec

Figure 12.6 The transaction processing profiles for the different components of the high-performance environment.

to DB2 rate. Although there is more than activity processing occurring on a systemwide basis (customers are opening and closing accounts, customers are changing their place of residence, and so on), the focus in terms of performance centers around activity processing. The normal activity processing includes cashing checks, determining balances, and receiving checks.

The two major sources of banking activities are ATMs and tellers. (In the background, run as a steady stream throughout the 24-hour day, the output of the MICR processing or automated check-clearing processing is delivered to DB2 for processing, but the stream from MICR can be regulated, unlike the stream of activities from ATMs and tellers).

The transaction arrival rate at different points in the system can be determined in several ways:

- If a conversion to DB2 is being done, existing arrival rates may be used.
- If another bank is willing to share its demographic and operational information, the arrival rate can be extrapolated.
- If estimates must be made on other than empirical data, then the analyst must factor into the estimated arrival rate the number of customers to be served, the banking habits of the customers, the growth of the population, and many other variables.

In any case, careful attention must be paid to *both* the total number of transactions to be managed and the peak-period transaction rate. The maximum transaction arrival rate is of interest even if the rate peaks sharply then subsides. The maximum rate achieved causes transactions to enqueue even if the rate is sustained for only a short period of time.

Rate 1 is time dependent on several factors: the time of day, the day of the month, and to a small extent, the month of the year. The peak rates are shown in Figure 12.6. During the evening the activity throughout the ATM-teller network is minimal. The average peak transaction arrival rate is 95 transactions per second with a peak around noon of a little over 200 transactions per second. During a peak day approximately 3.1 million transactions will be run.

Each ATM or teller transaction does not, however, result in a recordable activity for the bank. A recordable activity is one that changes the balance of an account in the system of record. One ATM transaction will verify an account's validity. Another ATM transaction will actually cause an account balance to change in the system of record. Still another ATM transaction will close off an ATM session with a cardholder when a session is made up of multiple transactions.

Furthermore, a fair number of ATM transactions will result in no recordable activity at all. An account holder may request a withdrawal of more than the account balance. Another account holder may merely want to verify account balance, and so forth.

In general, six ATM-teller transactions generate one recordable activity for the system of record that is maintained by DB2.

Rate 2 is for recordable activity only. All recordable activity is processed first from Fast Path to DB2, as all recordable activities are transacted against the system of record. As the balance is adjusted against all daily activities, the balance is returned to Fast Path. The first part of the cycle occurs from 6 P.M. until 3 A.M. at a peak rate of twenty-one transactions per second. The second part of the posting cycle occurs from 3 A.M. to 5:30 A.M. at a peak transaction rate of fifteen transactions per second.

About 510,000 activities per day need to be stored in the system of record. Throughout the day, Fast Path stores the activities for most accounts. (Some accounts are specially marked so that activity posting is done immediately by DB2. When DB2 refreshes data in Fast Path on a nightly basis, one piece of data stored by account is whether immediate posting should be done. The customer may request immediate posting, the account may be marked as a "trouble" account, the account may be a special upscale account, and so forth. However, no more than 2 percent of accounts are marked for immediate posting.) At the end of the business day, the DB2 accounts are posted based upon the stored transactions.

The peak processing time for posting is from 6 P.M. until 3 A.M. in the morning. During this time a steady twenty-one transactions per second are run into DB2. Note that, unlike ATM-teller processing where the peak-period rate fluctuated, the Fast Path DB2 rate does not fluctuate to any large extent. The transactions that flow into DB2 are highly designed; were they not designed, DB2 would not be able to process a workload peaking at twenty-one transactions per second. Each transaction accesses and updates one row of data—the row where the account balance is stored. The set processing of DB2 is severely constrained in that it is limited to the accessing and processing of one row. Consequently, the physical I/O incurred by each of the transactions being passed from Fast Path DB2

```
retrieve account n
add/subtract to balance
replace account n
  .    .    .    .
  .    .    .    .
  .    .    .    .
retrieve account n+1
add/subtract to balance
replace account n+1
  .    .    .    .
  .    .    .    .
  .    .    .    .
```

Figure 12.7 Typical activity processing in the DB2 environment from the Fast Path environment.

processing is minimized. Figure 12.7 illustrates the typical activity jobstream processing.

THE BANKING LIFE CYCLE

The full life cycle of a banking activity is shown by Figure 12.8.

In the morning an ATM customer withdraws $50. The Fast Path data base shows a balance of $400 at the time the request for withdrawal is made. The withdrawal is allowed. As the account is normal and does not require immediate passthrough (that is, immediate posting), it is held until the close of the business day. In the evening the $50 is transacted against the DB2 system-of-record data base, making the balance in the system of record $350. After all daily transactions are run, the Fast Path data bases are updated to reflect the new balances.

During the daytime, the DB2 processor is relatively untaxed, as far as activity run against it is concerned. Two moderately high volume activities occur during the day: post-MICR processing and customer statementing. One statement cycle is run each business day. (Actually once or twice a month, depending on the calendar, holidays, and the like, a statement cycle does not have to be run.) The only other major processing during the day occurs against account and customer activities, with the exception of DSS extract processing.

Depending on the workload and the day, some time is made available for DSS processing. The usual flow of activity for DSS processing is for extracts to be

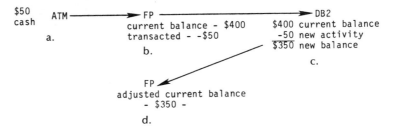

Figure 12.8 Life cycle of a banking activity: (*a*). 10:30 A.M. customer withdraws $50 from ATM; (*b*). 10:31 A.M. FP shows current balance of $400 and amount to be transacted of −$50; (*c*). 8:00 P.M. DB2 shows current balance of $400 and new balance of $350; (*d*). 3:30 A.M. FP updated with new balance of $350

run against DB2 data bases with the output of the extract being removed to another processing environment, such as the personal computer Lotus 1-2-3 spreadsheet environment. Very rarely does DSS analysis take place on the DB2 processor.

In general, the data flowing from the DB2 environment to the DSS environment flows directly into an atomic DSS data base. An atomic DSS data base provides a foundation for DSS processing. Atomic data bases store more archival data than that normally found in the DB2 environment and provide a basis for reconciliation of DSS processing when discrepancies occur. Furthermore, because atomic DSS data bases are removed from the DSS processor(s), the workload (as far as DSS processing is concerned) on the DB2 processor is alleviated. (For an in-depth discussion of the architecture and the environment of atomic DSS data bases, refer to my *Information Engineering for the Practitioner*.)

The Fast Path processor is a separate processor from the DB2 processor. The machines are physically separated, as are the data bases.

EXTENSIBILITY OF THE ENVIRONMENT

One of the features of the design of the example being described is the extensibility of the design. Should any component of the system become over-taxed with demands for resources, then more resources can be easily added. If an ATM begins to be heavily used, then two ATMs can be installed and attached to the Fast Path network. Should the ATM-teller link begin to reach its capacity, then another processor and another processing center can be installed. (In other words, a Central processing center can be added to the Northern and Southern processing centers if there is need for expanded processing power.)

Should DB2 processing become a bottleneck, DB2 data and processing can be separated onto two (or more) processors. However, long-term performance is not the only advantage of separating data by region. Availability of the system is enhanced as well. The multiple small data bases that store the system of record provide a high degree of uptime.

Should one small DB2 data base go down and become unavailable, only a fraction of the data of the processing center is affected. Furthermore, restoring a small data base takes less time and effort than restoring a large data base. The separation of the DB2 system of record data into small physical units enhances the availability posture of a system. The extreme flexibility and capacity of the configuration described pave the way for long-term high performance.

The high degree of extensibility of the environment depends on several factors:

- Programs access data based first and generically on region differences; that is, program code does not specifically code in only N or S, for example.
- The key structure of all data bases first accommodates the regional differences of the data.
- *All* types of keys are qualified, either directly or indirectly, on region.

- The partitioning of DB2 data is at the physical data base level, not at the DB2 partition level.

There is an anomaly in the above criteria for the example that has been developed. Although account and activity data are certainly oriented toward the regionality of data, customer data has no such orientation in its key structure.

One way to manage this anomaly is to add an extra byte for regionality in the customer key. Another way is to rely upon the account-customer relationship to position the data accordingly. For example, a customer opens an account in the northern part of the state. Both a customer record and an account record are established in the northern processing center, but only the key of the account explicitly shows in which center the data are domiciled.

Assuming that most of the processing for that customer will naturally occur in the Northern center, when the account-customer linkage or the customer-account linkage needs to be made, then there is no need to cross the MSC path from one processing center to the next. Only during the odd occurrences when activity first enters the processing network in a processing center other than the one where the data are domiciled (which should be only a small fraction of the time) will there be a need to switch processing from one center to the next.

The actual design of the DB2 tables for customer and account are of interest in that they show how the midlevel data model—the DIS (data item set)—is transformed into a physical data base design.

Accounts are divided into four classes: loans, savings, bankcard, and DDA (checking). Loans are further divided into three types: home loans, commercial loans, and other loans. The midlevel for the data model (showing keys and a few representative data elements) looks like Figure 12.9.

KEY STRUCTURES

The underlying key structure of the physical data bases are

ACCOUNT − ABCxxx . . . , A = region, B = cycle number, C = account type

LOAN ACCOUNT − ABCDxxx . . . , D = "L" signifying loan

HOME LOAN ACCOUNT − ABCDExxx . . . , E = "H" signifying home loan

COMMERCIAL LOAN ACCOUNT − ABCDExxx . . . , E = "C" signifying commercial loan account

OTHER LOAN ACCOUNT − ABCDExxx . . . , E = "O" signifying other loan account

SAVINGS ACCOUNT − ABCDxxx . . . , D = "S" signifying savings account

DDA ACCOUNT − ABCDxxx . . . , D = "D" signifying DDA account

BANKCARD ACCOUNT − ABCDxxx . . . , D = "B" signifying bankcard account

Using the DIS as a basis for physical design, DB2 tables are created, as shown in Figure 12.10.

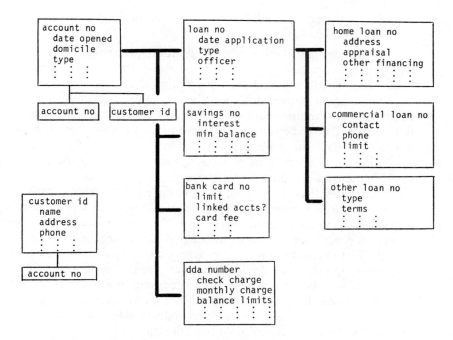

Figure 12.9 The midlevel data model for customer and accounts in the banking environment (showing keys and some data elements).

Note that even though account number is the key for the vast majority of the tables shown, the contents of the tables are mutually exclusive. Also note that the existence of the nonkey data depends directly on the existence of the type of key with which the data element is grouped.

From a performance perspective, it may make sense to group two or more tables together. However, the frequency of access of each of the tables shown will be such that denormalization will buy very little. The data, once created, is not often deleted, changed, or accessed (relative to other data). Consequently, denormalization does not apply to these tables.

DENORMALIZATION OF HIGH PERFORMANCE DATA

There is a place where the techniques of denormalization do apply, however. Consider the balance field. Every recordable activity will change the balance. On a nightly basis it is likely that each balance will be changed (or a large percentage of the balances will have had at least one recordable activity transacted against them during the day).

One design technique to handle balance processing (which has a very different set of processing and access criteria than other logically related account fields) is to create a special table(s) for balance. Figure 12.11 shows two tables used for high performance balance processing.

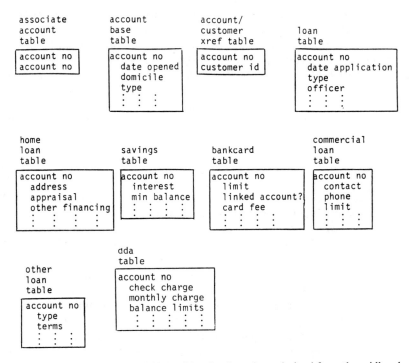

Figure 12.10 The physical DB2 tables that have been derived from the midlevel data model.

One table shows the balance table. There are only three fields in the balance table: account number (the key), balance, and conditions count. The other high performance table contains variable-length rows and three data elements: account number (the higher portion of the key), condition count (the lower portion of the key), and condition description. Most accounts do not have any conditions, and their condition count equals zero. When an account has unusual conditions, such as stop payment processing, immediate posting, special overdraft protection, and the like, the conditions are described in the second table.

On a nightly basis, the balance data are accessed and the balance is modified accordingly. No reference is made to condition as long as the condition count is zero. When the condition count is zero, then another access may need to be made

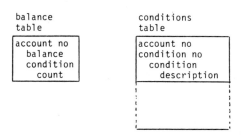

Figure 12.11 The high-performance balance tables.

to the condition table. In short, the nightly processing against account is brief and unencumbered by excessive I/O.

Furthermore, because of the small size of each entry in the balance table, many balance rows can be stored in a block. The tight packing of data increases the probability of a buffer hit, especially when the recordable activities can be preprocessed and sorted prior to nightly balance processing.

Note that the design of the high performance tables broke many of the rules of normalization. The need for high performance was greater than the need to adhere to logical design practices.

Summary

DB2 can be used in the high performance environment if DB2 is properly positioned. The system architect needs to be especially sensitive to the maximum transaction arrival rate, ensuring that the enqueue condition is not reached.

In addition the data base designer can prepare for future growth by ensuring that data can be split at the application level. Once data can be split at the application level, the processing workload can be split across multiple machines.

There are two ways data can be split: at the application level and at the system level (by the partitioning of data). Each technique has its advantages and disadvantages. However, if a default option needs to be chosen, the default of splitting data at the application level should be chosen.

The arrival rate of transactions coming into DB2 depends heavily on whether the transactions are designed or not. Undesigned transactions reduce DB2's maximum transaction arrival potential severely.

The splitting of data enhances not only performance but availability as well.

REFERENCES

Astrahan, M, et al, "System R: Relational Approach to Database Management," IEEE Computer Society: *Computer* 12 (5) May 1979.

Chen, P, *The Entity-Relationship Approach to Logical Data Base Design*, Data Base Monograph Series, No. 6. Wellesley, MA: QED Information Sciences, 1977.

Cheng, JM, Looseley, CR, Shibayima, A, and Worthington, PS, "IBM Database 2 Performance: Design, Implementation and Tuning," *IBM Systems Journal* 23 (2) 1984, G321-0076.

Codd, EF, "Normalized Data Base Structures: A Brief Tutorial," Proceedings of the 1971 ACM SIGFIDET Workshop on Data Description, Access and Control.

Date, CJ, *An Introduction to Data Base Systems*, Reading, MA: Addison-Wesley, 1974.

Fagin, R, "Normal Forms And Relational Database Operators," Proceedings of the 1979 ACM SIGMOD International Conference on Managment of Data. IBM Manual, "Database 2 Application Design and Tuning Guide," GG24-3004.

IBM Manual, "Database 2 Application Programming Guides" (TSO-SC26-4081, IMS-SC26-4079, CICS-SC26-4080).

IBM Manual, "Database 2 Concepts and Facilities," GC24-1582.

IBM Manual, "Database 2 Data Base Planning and Administration Guide," SC26-4077.

IBM Manual, "Database 2 General Information," GC26-4073.

IBM Manual, "Database 2 General Information Guide," GH24-5013.

IBM Manual, "Database 2 Guide to Publications," GC26-4111.

IBM Manual, "Database 2 Installation," SC26-4084.

IBM Manual, "Database 2 Introduction to SQL," GC26-4082.

IBM Manual, "Database 2 Operation and Recovery Guide," SC26-4083.

IBM Manual, "Database 2 Performance and Tuning Guide," GC24-1600.

IBM Manual, "Database 2 Reference," SC26-4078.

IBM Manual, "Database 2 Reference Summary," SX26-3740.

IBM Manual, "Database 2 Sample Application Guide," SC26-4113.

IBM Manual, "Database 2 System Monitoring and Tuning Guide," GG24-3005.

IBM Manual, "Database 2 System Planning and Administration Guide," SC26-4085.

Inmon, WH, and Bird, TJ, *Dynamics of Data Base*, Englewood Cliffs, NJ: Prentice-Hall, 1986.

Inmon, WH, *Effective Data Base Design*, Englewood Cliffs, NJ: Prentice-Hall, 1980.

Inmon, WH, *Information Engineering for the Practitioner*, New York: Yourdon Press, 1987.

Inmon, WH, *Information Systems Architecture*, Englewood Cliffs, NJ: Prentice-Hall, 1986.

Inmon, WH, "What Price Relational?" *ComputerWorld*, November 1984.

James, M, and Won, B, "Performance Management of Relational Database Systems," *INFOIMS*, Third Quarter 1983.

James, M, and Won, B, "Performance Management of Relational Database Systems: Part 2," *INFOIMS*, Fourth Quarter 1983.

Kroenke, D, *Database Processing: Fundamentals, Modeling, Applications*, Palo Alto, CA: Science Research Associates, 1977.

Looseley, C, "Resource Management in IBM DB2," Guide 65, Chicago, July 1986.

Looseley, C, "Measuring IBM Database 2 Release 2," *INFODB* 1 (2) 1986.

Martin, J, *Computer Database Organization*, Englewood Cliffs, NJ: Prentice-Hall, 1975.

PERKINSON, R, *Data Analysis: The Key to Data Base Design,* Wellesley, MA: QED Information Sciences, 1985.

WHITE, C, "DB2 Application Development: The Design Phase—Part 1," *INFOIMS,* First Quarter 1984.

WHITE, C, "DB2 Application Development: The Design Phase—Part 2," *INFOIMS,* Second Quarter 1984.

WIEDERHOLD, G, *Database Design,* New York: McGraw-Hill, 1977.

ZLOOF, M, "Operations on Hierarchical Data Bases," Proceedings of the NCC, 45, 1976.

INDEX

INDEX